PRAISE FOR ZERO TO A HUNDRED

"An eloquent and light-hearted story that will inspire you to take action on your ideas. Combining the wisdom of a purposeful businessman and the innocence of a dreaming teenager, *Zero to a Hundred* will give you the tools you need to build the life of your dreams. Truly inspirational."

—DAVE RUEL
Founder of Effic.co

ZERO TO A HUNDRED

My Millionaire Mentor's
Secrets to a Successful Life

MATHIEU FORTIN / JACK OUNDJIAN

Mention of specific companies, organizations, or authorities in this book does not imply endorsement by the authors, nor does mention of specific companies, organizations, or authorities imply that they endorse this book or its authors.

Copyright © 2017 Mathieu Fortin, Jack Oundjian. All rights reserved.

No part of this publication may be reproduced or transmitted in any form or by any means without the written permission of the authors.

ISBN: 978-0-9938736-4-5

For information on quantity discounts or on having this title customized for your company, please contact the authors via email at mathieu@mathieufortintv.com.

Requests for permissions should be directed to the authors directly via email at mathieu@mathieufortintv.com.

CONTENTS

Chapter 1 1

Chapter 2 13

Chapter 3 19

Chapter 4 25

Chapter 5 35

Chapter 6 41

Chapter 7 49

Chapter 8 55

Chapter 9 59

Chapter 10 67

Chapter 11 85

Chapter 12 97

Chapter 13 103

Chapter 14 119

Chapter 15 137

Chapter 16 147

Chapter 17	161
Chapter 18	163
About the Authors	167
Acknowledgments	169

CHAPTER 1

I'm not going to pretend like I saw the bright light at the end of the tunnel, but let me put it like this. When I finally got a chance to catch my breath and realize what had just unfolded in front of me, I knew I had screwed up... Big time.

In fact, I was kind of shocked. Not that the physical impact itself had been so brutal—it probably looked a lot worse from the outside—but my ego had definitely taken a big hit. Deep down, I felt sick. I was scared. Actually, *terrified* would probably be a better word to describe it.

See, one of the very first things they teach you in driving school is to never take your eyes off the road. Pure common sense, right? Say this to my 17-year-old self...

Sadly, it was now a little too late for me to catch up on this. Life lessons would have to wait.

I had let my attention run off at the worst possible moment. And obviously, I was the only one to hold accountable for this. Traffic lights had turned red in front of me. I was distracted. Next thing I knew, the horrific sounds of crushing metal were breaking the quietude of my imagination.

Needless to say, the beautiful Ferrari 458 I had been following for the past five minutes was now a complete loss. All because of me. What a mess...

I looked down at my hands; they were shaking. I was completely terrified by the idea of having to brave the other driver. I didn't have much of a choice, though; I had to make sure no one was injured on his side.

At that point, there was just too much going through my mind for me to handle. Although I had never been diagnosed with any anxiety troubles growing up, this particular moment made me feel like I had a big one. To top it off, the mentally unstable mobster stereotype wouldn't leave my mind as I was trying to picture the kind of man I'd have to face. It was bad. Very bad.

So, doing my best to gather all the courage I had left, I took a deep breath and jumped

Chapter 1

out of my car, heading straight towards the masterpiece I had just smashed.

I could feel my heart pounding in my chest, my palms getting wet. And unfortunately for me, things didn't get any better as I got closer to the car. In fact, with every step, things kept getting even worse.

The prancing horse ornament originally placed on the tail of the red beast was now embedded—literally—in the front grille of my car, while a taillight of the Ferrari had gone missing and at least three of its body panels would need to be replaced. Unbelievable...

But it wasn't the time, nor the place to let superficial details undermine me like that— although the damages I had caused alone would probably cost twice as much to fix than what I had paid for my car brand new.

Fortunately, the man was alone. I could see his shadow through the glossy window as I got closer to the car. It looked like he was trying to turn his wipers off, which were apparently going wild for no reason—some internal circuits had probably suffered from the impact.

As you would expect, his face stiffened as soon as he saw me. I took a step back and his door flung opened. In a clever move, the man slipped out of his seat and remained dead silent.

I bet most people wouldn't have noticed, but I had always had this fascination for fancy clothes and accessories. And judging by the way he was dressed, this guy was definitely into fancy things himself—wearing a dark blue Tom Ford suit, a white Eton shirt and a matching tie.

In silence, he stood in front of me for a second, looking at me straight in the eyes. But then, against everything I would've expected, he slowly loosened his tie and said:

"Everything all right?"

Physically, I guess I was okay. Psychologically, that was a whole other story. I mean, wasn't he angry? I had totaled his $350,000 car, after all. In addition, he was probably running late to an appointment or a Tuesday morning meeting because of me. I know for sure I would've been pissed... So, was he sorry for me? I had no idea; but questions were popping in my mind.

I simply nodded. And like he could read through the chaos of my thoughts, the man smiled and added:

"Now, why would I be angry? I mean, that's a lot of money you just blew right there." He pointed at the Ferrari. "But hey; that's it. Money comes and goes, my friend. That's how it works. Plus, I'm pretty sure you didn't do this on purpose, and quite frankly, I can't really see how being mad about it would make me feel any better.

"It sure won't bring the gloss back to my car!" he joked after taking a short pause. "And let's just say that I have faith in what life brings to me. I've always believed that everything happens for a reason. So I'm sure there's an explanation for this. There must be a good reason why our paths were meant to cross today..."

"Well, I ruined your car..."

"You did, and I'm sure there's a reason for that," he replied, looking at me with a smile. "But anyway, my name is Jack."

"I'm Mathieu," I said, shaking his hand.

"Nice to meet you, Math."

I nodded. "Let's say I would've preferred to meet you in other circumstances... I still want you to know that I'm really sorry about what happened."

"Oh! Looking at how pale your face is, I sure can imagine how sorry you are!" he laughed. He seemed to be in his mid-thirties. "Don't worry about it, things like that happen all the time. Besides, no one's injured; that's the important part, right?"

Once again, I simply nodded, trying to hide my embarrassment.

"Maybe we should get going with the insurance paperwork," added Jack.

"Yeah, sure."

We were standing right on the corner of Saint-Antoine and Square-Victoria—downtown Montreal. After grabbing a few blank forms from his glovebox, Jack took a quick look around and we both walked to one of the park benches lined up across the street.

Where was he from, eh? He obviously had a taste for fancy things. Yet, he just looked so young... There's no way on earth anyone could afford all that at such a young age—at least, that's what I had always believed. How did he manage to do it anyway? Was it even legal? And what about his credentials? I couldn't make up my mind about this guy.

Chapter 1

And frankly, the more I thought about it, the more confused I was.

We had been sitting next to each other for a couple of minutes now. And obviously aware that I had been staring at him for the past five minutes, wondering all sorts of things, Jack suddenly looked at me and said:

"You look like you could use some help... So, let me help you. *Pro bono*."

Confused, I took a quick look over my shoulder to make sure he was really talking to me. No doubt he was; we were the only ones around. Still, I had no idea what he was talking about, or what he meant by that.

"I appreciate the offer; that's very kind of yours, but I'm not sure I'm following you."

"Well, I'm not blind, you know! I can see it in your face since the second we've met; questions are eating you from the inside. So, what is it you're wondering? What I do for a living? Or maybe how you could get to do the same? What is it?" Jack replied, amused.

"Exactly... That's exactly what I've been wondering the whole time. But how did you..."

I paused, still puzzled. Meanwhile, Jack handed me a small piece of paper on which he had written what looked like a phone number, followed by an extension.

"Wait for a week—until next Tuesday—and then call this number," he continued. "I'll be expecting your call at 7 a.m. My assistant Melanie should pick up; she'll take care of you for the next step. When I feel like you're ready—and only then—we'll meet and I'll tell you everything you want to know. Deal?"

"Deal."

Now, *that* was pretty cool.

Jack nodded. And although we had never met before, I felt like he was right about me. I was at a point in my life where I needed some help to figure out certain things about my own existence and my career. And for some reason, this guy appeared to be the helping hand I had been looking for.

"May I ask you a question?" I said.

"Sure," Jack answered, back to his paperwork. "Go ahead."

"You seem to be really excited about all this; about this opportunity to share your knowledge with me. I don't want to come across as ungrateful, but we don't even know each other... So tell me; why? Why would you go out of your way to do this for a complete stranger?"

"Well, that's an interesting question. Perhaps you'll find it hard to believe, but let's just say that I recognize myself in you. When I first saw you, I didn't see *you*; the person I saw in front of me was the young and shy entrepreneur that I once was at your age. And that's when it hit me.

"Actually, the more I think about it, the more sense it makes! We met in these circumstances today for a very specific reason. I feel like it's now my responsibility to help and guide you. Just like my own mentors did for me when I first got into the corporate world, I feel like it's now my turn to pay it forward and pass on my knowledge to you.

"And you're right; we don't know each other yet. But I know how to recognize a pure intention," he slowly continued after pausing for a second. "My feelings tell me that you're a very passionate young man, filled with curiosity, ambitions and a lot of hidden talents.

"Now, correct me if I'm wrong, but my guts also tell me that you feel like your life is stuck in a dead end right now. You're seeking for answers, and I think this is precisely why we're both here today. I want to help, that's all."

"I don't really know what to say... Thanks, I guess. It means a lot. I feel like this is going to be the experience of a lifetime! And believe me, I'm very grateful for that. But all these things you seem to know about me, were they all so obvious?"

Purposely dodging my last comment, Jack took a quick look to the golden Rolex on his left wrist and suddenly got up to hand me the pile of documents.

"We'll have to talk about this a little later," he said. "I'm done with my part. You think you can go through the rest of it by yourself? I've got an appointment."

"Sure, no problem."

"Alright. Oh, and don't worry about my car," he added. "I'll send someone to pick it up in an hour or so."

We shook hands, and as he was walking away, phone up to the ear, Jack turned around in my direction and shouted:

"Tuesday morning, 7 o'clock! Be on time!"

I waved him. And two minutes later, as if nothing different than the usual had happened, the enigmatic character boarded a bus right next to the Square.

I smiled. Now, *that* was unexpected! Wasn't he supposed to have some sort of full-size SUV and a chauffeur coming to pick him up? Humility, I thought. I liked that. A second later, the crowded bus was gone.

I was now left all by myself in this surreal situation. Thirty minutes earlier, I was a 17-year-old boy with nothing but a confused mind and a dream. Now, I felt like the world was finally opening up to me. Nothing would be the same, ever again.

Sure, I still had that dream, but most importantly, I now felt like I had a way to get there. I had met a very generous man—a businessman, actually—who had offered me his knowledge, his advice and his experience on a silver platter. I didn't realize it at the time, but that alone was enough to make me one of the luckiest kids in the world!

CHAPTER 2

There I was, a whole week later. Tuesday morning, 7 a.m. That was our agreement. And for the past seven days, I had been thinking about this first 'official' meeting with Jack day in and day out, anticipating every second of it over and over again. But now that I was just a few hours away from the long-awaited moment, I've got to say, I was getting a little nervous.

Earlier that day, I had called Jack's office—right on time. What if he had changed his mind? I guess I didn't really know what to expect from this call, after all. Turns out that moments later, I had an appointment with my new mentor scheduled at 1 p.m. the same day.

When I finally got to our meeting point—Jack's office—the man I had met for the very first time a week earlier was already waiting for me outside, leaning against what appeared to be his ride for the day—a breathtaking black Bentley. No need to say, this was just like heaven for a car nut like me.

With his right hand, Jack waved me.

"Glad you came," he said, smiling. "We should probably get going. Come on, get onboard!"

"Wait, we're leaving?"

"Well, it's your call, but we have a whole bunch of stuff to cover. That said, I think it would probably best to avoid wasting time."

Apparently, this man would never cease to amaze me. I liked that. Everything was just going so fast with him. Yet, every move always seemed perfectly planned.

As soon as I got in the car, Jack turned on the ignition, waking up the beast. And in the sway of a glorious roar form the engine bay, we were hitting the road together. No doubt about it, this was something big for me; I was off to a new beginning.

Breaking the silence for the very first time since we had left Jack's office, I finally decided to go ahead and risk a first question.

"You told me last week that I would get all the answers to my questions 'when, and only when I'd be ready for them.' What exactly did you mean by that?"

Clearly expecting this question to come up sooner or later, Jack smiled.

"You know, when I was about six, my grandmother once told me a story," he replied. "And to be perfectly honest with you, it took me a little while to understand the lesson behind it. Looking back though, even after all these years, I still think this is one of the most valuable lessons I was ever taught. Want to hear it?"

Not knowing where this was going to take us, I simply nodded.

"It went as following," he continued. "Once upon a time, in a happy little town, there lived a very successful merchant. One day, the man told his oldest son: 'Boy, I think it's time for you to know what it's like to earn your own money. So tomorrow, I want you to wake up early, go out and work all day. You can sell fish or do whatever you want. But when I come home, you're going to show me how much money you've made.'

"The following morning, despite his father's instructions, the son woke up at 11 like he would on a typical day. And before he could even realize it, his laziness had also taken away the whole afternoon, leaving him with nothing but a beautiful sunset scenery to peek at. Panicked, the boy then ran to his mother, and asked her for an extra $20—it was time for plan B.

"Later that night, when his father got home, the son took the $20 bill out of his pocket and showed it to the merchant, claiming he had earned the money himself.

"'Alright,' replied the man. And without any warning, he then grabbed the bill and tossed it in the fireplace. Staring at the burning piece of paper, the merchant looked at his son and added: 'Son, you didn't earn those $20 today. Tomorrow is your chance to make things right.'

"Speechless, the boy went to bed that night thinking about this very moment. So, the day after, he got up at 6 AM. First thing in the morning, he went straight out to the lumber yard down the street and asked for a job, where he worked non-stop all day. And that night, when the boy got home after an exhausting day, he took the $5 he had made to his father's face and proudly said: 'Five dollars. That's what I made today.'

"Ice cold, the merchant took the money out of his son's hands. But this time, as he was about to throw it away like he had done the night before, his son came across and stopped him. 'Wait!' he said.

"Satisfied, the father gently gave the $5 bill back to his son and slowly added: 'See, *now* you know what it's like to earn something. These five dollars, no doubt you've earned them.'"

As he was pronouncing these last words, Jack pulled over.

"Obviously, there's also a much deeper meaning to this story," he noted. "Find it and that's when you'll know you're ready; that's where you'll find your first lesson."

"Wait a minute! That's it? I mean, what am I supposed to be looking for anyway?"

"You're smart," he said. "You'll figure it out."

Handing me a $20 bill, Jack looked at me and added:

"My plane is leaving for L.A. in about an hour. I have to go. Here; take a cab, go home and think about that. Next time we meet, I want you to have an answer. I know you'll figure it out."

I nodded. We shook hands and I stepped out of the car. There I was, standing by myself on the sidewalk with a $20 bill in hand, about ten miles away from where I had left my rental car.

As much as I hated to admit it, I was kind of overwhelmed by the situation. This guy was unbelievable. We had been together for the past 15 minutes or so, and I was already having a hard time keeping up with him.

When I thought he was going to teach me how to make my dreams come true and give me some advice—you know, what a mentor usually does—he basically gave me a blank homework and dropped me off.

I was a little confused. What kind of lesson was I supposed to be looking for anyway? I had no clue.

Sure enough, Jack wasn't messing around; he definitely wanted me to learn something there. I just had to figure out what exactly... And if I wanted to keep being a part of this journey as his protégé, I had to get started *ASAP*.

CHAPTER 3

Suddenly, it had become crystal clear. It all seemed so obvious now. Though, it's only several days later that I had finally found the answer to Jack's question. And on top of that, it had come up to me in a pretty unexpected fashion—in what I would describe as an *aha moment*.

The truth is; I had become obsessed with that question. And as I was eating breakfast that morning, almost ready to give up, that's when it all became so clear.

"You're always going to attach more importance to the things you've worked on; to value and appreciate what you've committed to build on your own!" I shouted as soon as Jack picked up the phone.

He laughed. "I knew you'd manage to think this through. You nailed it, buddy!"

"That's why you wouldn't give me any details, isn't it?"

"Sort of... Let's just say that I wanted you to understand the real value of what you're going to learn with me. I wanted to give you a little heads-up on what's waiting for you. Because you know; there's no point to taking someone's advice if you're not going to use it later on."

It all made perfect sense. And believe me, at that point, I was listening like never before. The guy was a genius—at least to me—and I had the privilege to be learning directly from him. How cool was that!

"Now, by pointing out the lesson in my grandmother's story, not only did you prove me that you cared, but most importantly, you showed me that you were ready to learn and make good use of my teachings," added Jack. "You showed me that you were ready for the next step."

"But does it really make a difference? I mean, I can't really see how this would apply to one's day-to-day life... You know, 'respect' is a very broad concept..." I interrupted him.

"Of course it makes a difference. See, the more you care about what you're doing, the more you want to succeed at it..."

"Yeah, this part I get, but how does it all translate in business or in life? What does it mean for the average guy, you know?"

"Well, for example, let's say I'm looking to hire a new general manager for one of my car dealerships. I have two candidates for the job. The first one has been working with me for the past five years; started as a salesman, and worked his way up to sales manager.

"The second candidate, on the other hand, has a fancy degree in management and a few years of experience in the automotive industry, but has never worked at my place. Who do you think is a better fit for the job? Who do you think will *care* the most?"

"The first one," I said.

"Right, and why is that? Because the guy has worked along with me to build the dealer's reputation for the past five years; he has made a lot of sacrifices to move up in the corporate ladder. Why? All because he cared."

"So, you're saying that the way he has valued his job, as well as the efforts he has put in over the past five years are what led him to strive for more, and thereby, to achieve more?"

"I'm saying that this is exactly how life's virtuous cycle works! When you can find something strong enough to keep your desires burning, you stick to it."

I remained silent for a second, like I still needed a little time to process all that information.

"Sounds good," I finally said. "But how exactly does it work? I mean, isn't there something missing between the part where all the efforts are deployed and the finale, where success is achieved? That part is still blurry to me."

"I thought you'd never ask!" answered Jack, obviously very excited about my question. "In fact, there is a whole bunch of steps you've got to take in order to succeed—whether it's in your personal life, at work or in anything else. And attaching importance to what you do is the very first one of them. Think of it like the tip of the iceberg. More specifically, it's the cornerstone that will eventually grant you access to the subsequent steps. Find it and you'll find the next key."

He paused, and I overheard him asking his assistant to clear his schedule for the afternoon.

"Alright, so here's what we're going to do next," he continued. "I think you're ready to hear what I have to say about self-discipline—which happens to be the second step. Hope you're not too busy after lunch, because we're going for a ride. I'll pick you up at 1 p.m.; be ready!"

"I'll be waiting," I slowly replied. "See you then!"

No doubt about it; Jack definitely had a lot to teach. And as luck would have it, I also felt like I had a lot to learn.

CHAPTER 4

For the past few hours, I had been waiting for the man to show up as if my life depended on it. Because one way or another, this meeting *was* going to have an impact on my life. With that in mind, needless to say that my morning had been totally unproductive.

Right on time, the roar of Jack's Bentley first announced his arrival. And just as I was trying to find my sunglasses, the doorbell rang.

"Ready to take on the first day of the rest of your life?" asked Jack as soon as I opened the door. He was wearing a broad smile, showing his obvious enthusiasm.

"You bet I am!"

We shook hands, and Jack added:

"Alright, then let's get going."

If I remembered feeling rather shy and quiet in our first meeting, now was a whole different story. In fact, it was quite the opposite this time—I felt like we had known each other forever.

The atmosphere in general was just different, more casual. Jack was wearing a nice pair of jeans and a white shirt. The sun was shining outside, the breeze was warm; perfect for rolling down the windows. Everything seemed into place this time. Everything just felt right.

"So why don't you tell me a little more about yourself?" said Jack, breaking the silence.

Of all the questions I thought he would ask, I wasn't expecting this one.

"Just start with the beginning," he added.

"Well, I've always been more of a solitary kid—which I think is due to the fact that I grew up as an only child. Over the years, I've developed a fleeting interest for all sorts of things, going from a project to another without really knowing what I was doing.

"And although I know I'd love to become a successful writer, I feel like I'm in a dead end right now… I know I'm only 17 and I still have plenty of time to figure it out, but I've never been the type of guy to wait for things to happen on their own; I like to make things happen. And to be honest, I don't know what I want anymore, and it freaks me out."

"A writer, eh? That's awesome! And as for the rest, no need to worry. I'll help you think this through when the time is right; just don't try to beat the clock, alright?"

I nodded.

"Let me tell you something," he said. "Whether you're still confused or you know exactly what you're going after, know that the knowledge I'll be sharing with you can be applied in just about any situation.

"I guess what I'm trying to say is that regardless of who you've been, who you are and who you'll become, these principles will evolve and mature with you. No matter what happens, you'll always be able to rely on them to find the answers you need."

"And what principles are we talking about exactly?"

"Not so fast! First of all, remember this morning on the phone when I told you that showing respect for what you do was actually the very first step to success? Well, the only way you can get to show that kind of respect is by *earning* instead of *getting*. That's the only way. Once you understand that, the next step is to become an absolute master of self-discipline."

He paused for a second, and made a left turn.

"People tend to perceive the word 'discipline' as rude or negative sometimes," Jack added. "If you don't like the term, you can always swap it with 'consistency,' or even 'structure.' But the truth is; there's really nothing negative about self-discipline. I mean, it's a tool; one that's going to provide you with a desire to push your own limits and succeed. So, tell me; what's negative about that?"

"I get your point, but why is that even an issue? Why are there so many people misconceiving what discipline is about in the first place?"

"Honestly, I have no idea... Maybe they think of it as a form of repression or something. But whatever the reason, you can't expect to succeed with such a mindset. You'll have to change that perception for yourself if you ever want to have any success."

I nodded.

"So, there's a few basic principles you should be aware of to begin with," he resumed. "The first one being that routine creates habits. In fact, through all the small things we do every once in a while, we're creating habits.

"Some of them are good, while most of them are actually harmful. That's just how it goes; people tend to create bad habits way more often than they create good ones."

"Really?"

"Yup. Why? Because creating new brain patterns generally takes two things; consistency and time. Every new habit needs that, good or bad. However, creating a *good* habit often requires you to overwrite an old one—a bad one—which calls for an extra load of discipline and effort."

Seeing that I had a hard time following, Jack went on with an actual example.

"People who smoke two packs a day didn't start this overnight. I bet they probably smoked once at a party, twice maybe, and that's how their body got used to the chemicals. They've simply let temptation take care of what we often see as the 'harder' part, also known as the *consistency* part. And next thing you know, they're burning two packs a day!"

"They've created a habit," I said.

"Plain and simple. See, there's nothing really hard in the process of creating a habit. Most of the time, external influences like people or addictive agents will even take care of the consistent effort for you—how clever.

"But now, let's say you want to quit smoking. In other words, let's say you want to get rid of this harmful habit and replace it with a better one. Well, that's a little more complicated. Why? Because in addition to creating the new habit, you also need to take care of the addiction... And let's be honest, that's going to take a tremendous amount of self-discipline, especially to keep your effort consistent despite the addiction.

"Long story short, this kind of progress doesn't happen just like that. Big changes don't occur overnight; they're the result of many small changes put together through time and consistent effort."

On the side of the road, I saw a sign indicating that we were heading south. Frankly, I didn't really care. I was absorbed by what Jack had to say; all I wanted was the rest of the principles.

Chapter 4

"Here's another example," he continued after a short pause. "Perhaps this one is going to make more sense to you. Let's say I'm looking for a babysitter. If I offered you one penny a day for a month, but I doubled the amount every single day, would you take the job or you'd rather get a $5000 check upfront for the whole month? Think about it."

There's absolutely no way it could be that easy... Not with him. There was trick.

"I'd go for the penny," I finally said.

He laughed, looking at me.

"Well, I sure hope so! On the 31st day alone you'd be making over ten million dollars! Pretty well-paid for a few hours of babysitting, eh?"

"But how is this even—"

"That, my friend, is the beauty of the compound effect," he interrupted me. "Think of it as an old train that takes off; of course it's going to be very slow at the beginning. But once it goes full speed, it becomes very hard to stop. And gradually, this is the kind of momentum you want to create in your life.

"Even the smallest details have the power to make a change once they're put together as a whole. And it's by working consistently on these small changes that you'll be able to make big changes; that's how you'll reach out to the level of success you deserve."

Now, that was a pretty big *aha moment* for me right there. You know, as a naturally optimistic guy, I had always had this kind of fascination for big dreams and crazy goals. But so far, I had never really stopped to think about how I could actually get to achieve these goals.

The mere possibility of eventually 'making it' seemed to be enough to get me going at the time. I would just take action and hope that everything would turn fine. But I really had no idea what I was doing; I was trying to hit the bull's eye with a blindfold. At least, that's what it felt like.

And as a result, well, I'd feel disappointed most of the time. I mean, who wouldn't? And at this point, I would simply move on to the next goal or the next project.

So, for all these years, I had been repeating this pattern over and over again, *hoping* to see my dreams come true instead of actually *making* them come true. In other words, through my attempts to achieve everything at once, I would end up doing nothing.

And don't get me wrong; my goals were not the problem. My attitude towards them was. If I had seen them as a series of small achievable steps instead of treating them as one big and unattainable dream, chances are that I would've been much more inclined to succeed.

"But here's the part I don't get," I thought out loud. "If all these little actions we take on a daily basis are so subtle, how do we know if we're progressing or not? Don't you think it's a lot easier to stay consistent when you can actually see the progress?"

"It is, and that's why you've got to keep track of your progress," replied Jack. "Like anything else, the results you get from the actions you take can be measured and tracked.

"Take a look at professional athletes, for example. They track everything. The calories they eat, how long they sleep, how much time they spend on training; everything. Of course, performance improvements don't happen overnight. But with all this data, they're able to clearly identify both their strengths and weaknesses. And, in the long run, that's how they can adjust their strategy and improve on the field."

"In other words, tracking progress allows you to make better decisions and be more efficient in your actions, is that what you're saying?"

"Pretty much! I mean, let's say you want to learn how to play piano. On day one, you might be able to align a few notes at best. But if you're consistent, you keep practicing every day and you keep tracking your progression, who knows; you might be able to play a whole symphony in just a few weeks.

"The point is—and I can never stress this enough—the more you focus on creating good habits and tracking what you're doing—"

"The better my chances of finding success," I said, completing his thought.

"You got it, buddy. Small actions lead to big changes."

I nodded. A peaceful atmosphere was now filling the the car, as we were both silent. And for the first time in my life, I felt like I was about to find my way in this world. I was ready to take on the challenge.

CHAPTER 5

I still had no idea where Jack was taking me. We were cruising on the highway now, passing slow drivers like a cannonball. The past 20 minutes had been very enlightening, and all I could think of at that point was self-discipline.

According to my new mentor, self-discipline was the backbone of success. No matter what you do, your brain is creating new patterns and developing new habits.

And thus, in order to be successful, you want to create good habits; this is where self-discipline comes into play. The sooner you become consistent and coherent in your actions, the sooner you'll succeed. It really wasn't that hard to understand.

It all made sense in theory, but I still felt like I was missing something.

"Here's what I keep wondering," I finally said. "I understand how important it is to create good habits and stay consistent in your actions, that's fine. But how do you manage to actually maintain this level of discipline on an ongoing basis? I mean, don't we all want to quit at some point? Don't we all have our ups and downs?"

"Well, that's a good question," answered Jack after a moment. "I guess this is going to be our next topic of discussion."

"Great! So, what's the secret sauce?" I asked, obviously very happy with his answer.

"First of all, there's no secret sauce. You need to take this idea out of your head. Successful people don't take shortcuts. There's no such thing as shortcuts in business—or in anything else, for that matter. All you have to do is to follow the steps."

"Oh, I didn't mean to—"

"Don't feel sorry," said Jack, interrupting me. "I just want you to understand that success is the product of calculated actions. If you're going to succeed, if that's your plan, you've got to be willing to put in the work.

"Remember the story I told you the other day; my grandmother's story? You've got to show some respect for what you do. And then, success will come to you."

"You're right, I shouldn't have brought that up."

"No, I'm glad you did. That's how you learn."

I nodded.

"Now, to answer your question," he continued. "There are indeed a few things you can do to make sure you don't run out of self-discipline. The first one would be to advertise your goal."

"To advertise my goal?" I replied, intrigued. "What's that supposed to mean?"

"Well, here's how it works. I'm sure you know this, but most people tend to give a lot of credit to what others think or say about them. In fact, peer pressure is known to be one of the most influential factors on how a person acts and behaves.

"Does it mean it's right? Of course not. But it's reality. And as long as people stay unaware of their power to change things—or as long as they keep denying it—things are going to remain the same. So, in the meantime, why not take advantage of this reality why we still can?"

"By advertising our goals?" I asked.

"Exactly. Think about this for a second; I'm pretty sure you've already given up on a project or an idea after the first few hurdles. We've all been there at some point. You know why?"

I shook my head. "I have no idea."

"Because we keep our goals to ourselves. That's why. Let me ask you this; would you have done the same thing if a hundred people knew about your goal? Do you think you would've quit with the same peace of mind? I don't think so. I think your ego would've gotten in the way.

"It's easy to give up on your dreams when nobody else is watching; when no one knows what you're up to. But when you go out every day and get asked about your projects by your friends and coworkers, quitting then becomes a lot harder for the ego.

"You don't want this to be the go-to option when you're facing resistance; you don't want it to be easy for you to give up. And advertising your goal makes it harder. A lot harder."

"So, it's all about pride and ego, eh?"

"I guess you could put it that way, but I think it goes beyond that," said Jack. "In fact, it's also a matter of finding the right help.

Chapter 5

You know, if I asked you to think of someone who's had massive success on their own—with no help whatsoever—chances are that you wouldn't be able to answer, would you?"

Before I could even put a word in, he continued.

"That'd be understandable, because frankly, there's no such thing. Everybody needs help at some point, and the more you advertise your goals, the better your chances of finding someone willing to help you. It's a numbers game."

"Makes sense," I said.

"Of course it does! Just go out there and spread the word. Someone might know someone; you never know what could come out of this."

I nodded.

On the dashboard, the clock was showing 2:05 PM. Our conversation had me so absorbed that I had completely lost track of time.

"There's a McDonald's a few blocks away. I'll grab a milkshake; you want something?" asked Jack.

What a good idea. "Sure, I'll have one too!"

A minute later, we headed straight to the restaurant's drive-thru where Jack ordered two large chocolate milkshakes. With the same enthusiastic smile he was wearing an hour earlier on the footstep of my door, the man handed me one of the paper cups and said:

"Cheers!"

CHAPTER 6

The sun was shining outside, and Jack had parked the car so we could both get out and enjoy the rest of our shake at one of the picnic tables lined up nearby.

"Another way to stay disciplined and motivated would be to surround yourself with the right people," he then said, interrupting my thoughts.

Confused, I frowned. "I thought I was supposed to work on myself, not on the whole town…"

"Make no mistake; this is still a very important part of the process. The people around you do have a tremendous impact on you as a person. And surrounding yourself with the wrong people could jeopardize not only your success, but also your personal growth."

"Really?"

Jack nodded. "Here's why," he continued. "It's been proven that we humans tend to become just like the five people we spend most of our time with. I'm sure you've noticed that wealthy and successful people always seem to hang out together. That's because like-minded people tend to attract one another."

"And what exactly is that supposed to mean?" I asked, still not entirely sure what to think.

Without flinching, Jack kept on going.

"Have you ever heard of the old adage 'misery loves company'?"

"I guess so. Why?"

"Well, it basically means that negativity attracts negativity," he explained. "So, regardless of the amount of time and effort you put in to keep a healthy mindset, stay positive and maintain a high level of self-discipline, it's all of no use if you can't stay away from toxic people."

I remained silent.

"You know," Jack continued. "Over the course of your life, you'll be continually asked to make decisions. And choosing who you want to be friends with and who you want to be working with happens to be one of those decisions.

"Now, because of the way we like to interact with others, we tend to bond with people who share similar interests. And it makes perfect sense. However, what I've come to notice over the past few years is that we also tend to attract men and women who have a similar attitude."

"So, that would explain why successful people seem to 'attract' one another; because of their attitude."

Jack smiled.

"As crazy as it may sound, we humans like to connect with people that are just like us. We like to see a reflection of ourselves in others. So yeah, attitude plays a very important role in that equation.

"It's true for the wealthy and successful, but also for everyone else on this planet. We all end up being just like the five people we spend the most time with. That said, if your goal is to set yourself free of debt, you might want to make friends that are already financially set. If you plan on getting fit, you should probably start hanging out with people who exercise regularly. You get the idea?"

I nodded. "It definitely makes sense."

"Good. Now, let me ask you this; if I want to learn how to make a million dollars, should I take advice from the broke man or the rich man? Although it might seem pretty obvious when you put it this way, people tend to forget about the importance of carefully choosing who they listen to.

"If you ask me, I personally like to take advice only from people who have already achieved the kind of results that I want—that's how I work. With that in mind, I think the same principle also applies when it comes to choosing who you surround yourself with.

"And don't get me wrong, I'm not saying that negative folks are bad people. But the way I see it, you need to surround yourself with the ones who can help you grow and move forward. And unfortunately, the defeatists are just downright toxic for your growth.

"I mean, think about this; what do you think would happen to all your goals and your dreams if all your trusted friends and relatives told you 'it's impossible' or 'you can't do that'? Chances are that you would end up believing these fallacies and you'd give up... Because remember; we become just like the five people we spend the most time with."

"So, what exactly are you suggesting?" I asked, intrigued. "That I start being more careful as to who I allow in my inner circle? Based on what criteria? I mean, I get the idea, but don't you think it sounds a little arbitrary?"

"What I'm saying is that you can monitor and adjust certain variables in your daily life to make sure you get to meet the right people. In other words, you can sometimes make the right things happen just by being at the right place at the right time.

"And I'm not talking about manipulating people or adopting any other lousy behaviour—far from that. However, I do believe that we have a certain control over who we meet and interact with—once again, simply by making sure we're at the right place at the right moment."

I slowly nodded. "And how do you do that?"

"It's actually a lot easier than you would think," Jack answered. "All you have to do is to pay close attention to where you spend your time. For instance, you probably wouldn't hang out in a pub if you had just checked out of rehab.

"Well, similarly, if you're looking to become financially free, your first move should be to look for places where you actually have a chance to meet financially independent people. So, where would that be? At your local country club? Or maybe at a charity event? Just do the math and you'll figure it out."

He took a deep breath and looked at me.

"You want to surround yourself with a handful of people that are going to help you grow and become who you really want to be," added Jack. "And by doing so, chances are that you'll end up wanting to achieve greatness for yourself. That's why surrounding yourself with like-minded people is so important. It opens your horizons to a whole new world of possibilities."

Jack was right. I knew I would probably have to surround myself with the right people if I ever wanted to succeed as a writer. I also knew I would probably need to find myself a mentor within that industry as well; I guess I just didn't know how pivotal that was.

Chapter 6

So, there we were, enjoying what was left of our milkshakes at one of the many picnic tables lined up on the grass. The sun was still shining, and a soft breeze was now filling the place.

After taking a quick look at his watch, Jack suddenly got up and slowly headed back to the car. It was time to leave.

CHAPTER 7

We both remained silent for a while on the way back home. It's only several minutes later that Jack finally decided to speak up.

"I've been thinking," he said. "And there's still one more thing you could do to help maintain a high level of self-discipline and motivation. Can you guess what it is?"

I took a few seconds to think about it. "I honestly have no idea… But I'm listening."

"It's pretty simple; no matter what you do, you have to be willing to do whatever it takes to bring it as far as you possibly can. In other words, whenever you start a new project, you've got to commit yourself to leading it to term—or at least, as far as you can."

He paused for a second, staring at the road. "And to do so, the first thing you'll need to figure out is how to get familiar with failure."

"Wait a minute," I interrupted him. "What exactly is that supposed to mean? Is this some kind of joke? Because in case you haven't noticed, failing isn't fun... at all."

"Don't get me wrong; I'm not trying to make you believe that failing is fun. You're absolutely right; it sucks. What I want you to understand, however, is that what you see as 'failure' is not an end in itself.

"So yeah, failing will most definitely piss you off at first—no one likes that. But then, it's your responsibility to take a step back and figure out a way to get over that frustration. And believe me when I say this; getting familiar with failure and liking it are two very different things.

"Now, I'm not asking you to like it. But either way, I can guarantee you that you will eventually face some challenges. And to me, learning how to properly deal with failure simply means not letting it affect you—or if you prefer, not letting it stand between you and your goals. That's it."

I had to admit, his explanation actually sounded a lot better than I thought it would.

"And let me ask you this," added Jack. "Why do you think you're so afraid of failing?

Chapter 7

I'll tell you why; because it makes you uncomfortable. That's the only reason."

I nodded in silence, still trying to process all this new information.

"The way I see it," he continued. "A failure is really nothing more than a 'no' in disguise. When it happens—because you and I both know it will—your first reaction should be to stay focused on your goal. Then, you just get your shit together and move on.

"Has a simple 'no' ever killed anyone? I don't think so. And one thing's for sure, achievers don't hold themselves down over a little setback, because they know better than anybody that there's no such thing as a permanent failure."

I looked at him in disbelief. "I just don't get it... I mean, I know from personal experience that failing can be particularly hard sometimes. So tell me, how do you move on so easily?"

"Well, I guess it's a matter of perspective. No one ever said that you couldn't be successful after failing five, ten or a hundred times in a row. That's a misconception that we have. You *can* fail, and you probably *will* fail. That's why in order to stay motivated, you've got to learn how to detach yourself from the frustration of being defeated. That's what's going to keep you going."

I nodded. Jack's argument made perfect sense.

"Now, we talked about the importance of tracking your progress," he continued. "But the truth is; you'll never be able to do so if you can't lead your projects to term. That's a fact. I mean, how can you improve a result if you don't know what the result is in the first place? You just can't.

"So, always make sure you finish what you start. Otherwise, you won't ever be able to know what did or didn't work, and I can promise you that sooner or later, you'll end up in a dead end."

"And in order to lead my ventures to term, I guess I'm going to need to make sure that failure doesn't get in my way, is that right?"

Jack looked at me, satisfied. "Correct. You would never see hockey players give up after the first period because their team is losing 2-0. Why? Because although they might have missed a few opportunities to score at the beginning of the game, the players are perfectly aware that *nothing is not over until it's over*.

"Meaning that, if you want a chance to win in life, you've got to overcome the challenges as you face them, and finish what you start. Because at a certain point in your life, all these things were worth being finished to you. Otherwise, chances are that you wouldn't have started them in the first place. So, when you start something, make sure you commit yourself to finishing it."

"Sounds fair enough," I noted with an approving gaze.

We had been cruising around for a while now, and apparently, we were already a few blocks away from my where I lived. Time was flying by so fast with this man. It was fascinating. It just seemed like I had so much to learn from him.

"It's been really nice catching up with you today," said Jack as he pulled over. There it was again; the same warm smile he was wearing a few hours earlier.

"I've had a good time, too! And again, I want you to know that I am so grateful for what you're doing here. Thank you so much."

"Well, I'm glad you appreciate it. Let's keep in touch. And by the time we meet again, I'd like you to take some time to really think about everything we've talked about today. Take some time to let that sink in."

"Of course," I quickly answered, shaking his hand. "I will."

He nodded.

"Oh, and one last thing!" said Jack as I was walking away. "Next time, I want you to come up with an explanation on why mistakes play such an important role in success."

"Consider it done!" I shouted, waving at him.

Seconds later, Jack was gone, leaving me once again with a very simple—and yet not so easy—homework for our next meeting. This time, however, the answer I was looking for was literally lying right in front of me...

CHAPTER 8

What an afternoon. Probably one of the most eye-opening moments of my entire life.

Now, Jack wanted me to come up with an explanation on why mistakes play such a key role in success, but I honestly had no idea where to start digging.

When I was a kid, my parents used to tell me about how I should always keep my head high and do my best to overcome adversity. But why? I mean, it seemed like the right thing to do and I knew they were right, but I had never really taken the time to stop and think about it before...

I needed some fresh air. Outside, the breeze was still warm and cozy, but the sun had lost a bit of its shine; the perfect combination for a quick walk around the block.

People were returning from work, and slowly, cars were starting to roll down the street. The landscapers working at our neighbors' house had already left, allowing summer camp buses to drop off their young passengers. And soon, jiggling kids were all over the place.

On my end of the street, though, the atmosphere didn't feel so pimping. My mind was filled with all these questions, and yet I couldn't seem to find the answers I was looking for.

Feeling my thoughts drifting away, I looked down and noticed a gigantic anthill emerging from a curb joint. Ants had always fascinated me for some reason; how could such tiny creatures carry more than eight times their own weight? That was just mind-boggling.

About ten feet away, two of them caught my attention. With a significant amount of effort and determination, the two ants had somehow found a way to carry the shell of another insect, about five times their size. And against everything I would've expected, it's by observing these two little ants at work that I finally understood the deeper meaning of Jack's latest lesson.

Every time their load would fall down, their first reaction would be to try and pick it up again, this time using a different technique. Instead of doing the same thing over and over, they were learning from their mistakes. Now, if that's not a sign of intelligence, I truly wonder what it is.

So, according to Jack, why was failure such a critical step in one's journey to success? I had the answer right in front of me; because mistakes give you an opportunity to learn. They allow you to acquire new skills, and to find all the bits and pieces of knowledge you need to succeed.

When I looked at the two ants, I saw Jack's words in action. Despite all the challenges they ran into, the bugs never gave up on their ultimate goal. Instead, they revisited their strategy with each and every setback, learning from their mistakes along the way until they eventually found a way to make it work.

As silly as it might sound, this moment in its simplicity was a true revelation for me. For the first time, I felt like I had made a giant step forward. Was that the compound effect starting to kick in? I had no idea. But one thing's for sure; the more I learned, the less I felt I knew.

Happy with the way things had turned out, I smiled and slowly headed back home.

CHAPTER 9

Unfortunately for me, Jack was still a busy man, after all. And thereby, I would have to wait a few more weeks before I could pick his brain again. On the positive side, the wait reminded me of just how blessed I was to actually have him as a mentor.

In the first few days that followed our most recent meeting, Jack and I exchanged a couple of text messages in which my instructions were clear; I had to wait for his call.

Two seemingly endless weeks went by before I heard back from the man. But on the first Wednesday of August, I finally got a call.

"Things have been pretty crazy around here lately," said Jack on the phone. "I wish I could've called you earlier. But you know the saying; in the midst of chaos, there is also opportunity!"

"No worries. I'm glad we finally get to catch up!"

"Me too," he slowly answered. "So, I'm taking Friday off, and I was thinking maybe we could get together and pick up where we left off. What do you think?"

"Of course! That'd be great."

I could hear the clicking of his keyboard in the background. "Alright, buddy. I'll pick you up at nine; there's something I want to show you. And what's up with the homework I gave you? Have you managed to find the answer yet?"

"I've been on it the second I left your car!"

He laughed. "Fair enough," added Jack in a chuckle. "Can't wait to hear what you have to say about that. See you on Friday!"

Two days later at 8:55 AM, I was standing on the curb in front of my parents' house, like a school kid waiting for his bus. I had been anticipating this moment for several weeks now, listing all my questions on a piece of paper.

And since I was expecting to see the Bentley coming around the corner, you can imagine how thrilled I was when instead I heard the screaming engine of Jack's Ferrari down the street.

Seriously, what a badass car!

Chapter 9

"There you are," said Jack through the open window. "Come on in."

Despite a clear attempt to control my emotions, I just couldn't hide my enthusiasm. As soon as I closed the door, Jack stepped on the accelerator and the car took off, making me feel like I was sitting in a rocket.

"So tell me," began Jack after I had a chance to calm down. "Why is it that failure plays such an important role in the way we succeed?"

"Because mistakes are a great way to learn, and I think learning is what ultimately leads to success," I replied in a surprisingly confident tone—one that I had never used in any of our previous conversations.

"I thought this one would've been a bit more challenging..." added Jack with a smile. "I can't say it's much of a surprise either; I was right about you, Math. Good job!"

I smiled back. "Thanks. I'll take that as a compliment, but how about you get a little more into the details now? I mean, I get the idea, but I'd like to hear what you have to say about it."

"Well first off, I genuinely believe that no one should ever be afraid of failing," said the man before making a left turn. "Why? Because unlike what you've been taught in school, mistakes are actually good. As weird as it may sound, I really think that mistakes are your gateway to a brighter future—given that you know how to use them properly, of course."

Still not entirely sure what he meant by that, I slowly nodded.

"Think about this for a second," Jack went on. "What if you could draw a lesson out of every mistake you'll make from now on? Don't you think all that knowledge would eventually add up to help you succeed? Don't you think all these lessons would be profitable in the long run?"

"When you put it this way..."

"People who focus on the end result more than on the journey itself tend to adopt a negative attitude towards mistakes," he said, interrupting my thought. "Yet if you look at it closely, being wrong is merely an opportunity to take a step back, learn, and try again with an improved strategy—like a second chance, basically.

"In other words, failure isn't an end in itself; it's more of a reality check, if you will. That's why focusing on the journey rather than the goal is, in my opinion, the best thing you can do. Believe me, that's going to help you deal with failure a lot better than just focusing on the results alone. Because remember; success is about progress, not perfection."

I gave him a puzzled look. "So the bigger and the faster you fail, the bigger and the faster you succeed, that's what you're saying?"

"Given that you're able to draw a lesson out of every mistake you make along the way, then yeah, that's exactly what I'm saying," replied Jack.

"And how come nobody seems to be aware of this?"

"Two words: formal education. It all starts there, no need to look further than that."

"What do you mean?" I asked, still confused.

"Well, don't get me wrong here. I may not be a big fan of how our current educational system reprimands failure, but I'm a strong advocate of instruction and knowledge. That said, I strongly disagree with the way we're dealing with mistakes in the traditional system.

"Schools as we know them are teaching our kids that being wrong is wrong. Any wonder everyone seems to be so afraid of failing when they grow up... How can you expect people to focus on the positive elements of failure when they've always been told not to make mistakes in the first place?"

As much as I hated to admit it, he was right; that didn't make any sense. Once again, I felt really glad I had him to teach me that kind of stuff.

"Anyway," added Jack, dragging me out of my thoughts, "my point is that sooner or later, you will fail; we all do. And when that happens, you have to be prepared to take advantage of the situation and seize the opportunity to learn from it.

"Otherwise, you'll just repeat the same mistakes over and over again without even knowing why. And trust me, you don't want that! Because in order to succeed, you've got to be able to figure things out on your own. And for this to happen, well, you need to start

Chapter 9

treating every mistake you make as an opportunity to learn."

Jack paused for a second, and as we entered what seemed to be the Mount Royal Park, he looked at me and said:

"We're here."

CHAPTER 10

A few minutes later, the car was parked and we were both walking up the hill; me following him without really knowing where he had planned to take me and why. I genuinely had no idea what to expect.

"There's something I need to show you," Jack began. "We're almost there."

About twenty minutes later, when we finally reached the top of the mountain, he stopped and invited me to join him on one of the park benches facing the city. The hardest climbs often yield the prettiest views, they say. Well, this one was no exception.

I was having trouble catching my breath, but the view was definitely worth it. Although I had grown up in the neighborhood, I had never really taken the time to come up there and admire the beautiful landscapes Montreal had to offer. In fact, I had never really heard all that much about this place until then.

In front of us, the sun was reflecting on the buildings, and the soft breeze was bringing leaves to life in the trees. From a distance, everything in the city looked so chaotic, and yet so calm at the same time. For once, I felt like I was living in the present; no worries, just the *here* and *now*.

"Pretty cool, eh?" said Jack, interrupting my thoughts.

Trying to soak up as much as I could from this place, I took a deep breath. "Inspiration at it's purest form. I love it."

"That's exactly why I brought you here. Ready for another lesson?"

With an unusual feeling of confidence, I nodded.

"Alright," he continued. "So, I'm sure you've already heard about this, but becoming great at something is essentially nothing more than a mind game. I know it sounds cheesy, but like Henry Ford used to say; *whether you think you can or you think you can't, you're right*. And as it turns out, he was 100% right about that."

"In other words, it's your attitude towards a challenge or a project that dictates the kind of outcome you get, is that what you're saying?"

"At least, the better part of it, yes. You know, I really do believe that we were all born with the same opportunity in life; the opportunity to create and live our own life. And yet, very often, our limiting beliefs seem to take away this freedom of ours, leaving us with a mere feeling of helplessness towards the events that occur in our own lives..."

"And what exactly are these beliefs?" I asked, interrupting him.

"Well, there's a whole bunch of them. First, there's the infamous 'Others can do it, but I can't because I'm poor, I'm not good enough, etc.' Then, you also have people who claim that they can't do it because they don't know where to start, or because they don't think they deserve to be successful; you know, the usual B.S.

"Possibilities are virtually endless here. And don't get me wrong; they're all good reasons not to move forward, I'll give you that. But are they good enough to prevent you from living the life of your dreams? If so, just keep on living your life like you always have. But if not—which is far more likely—then you must get rid of those limiting beliefs."

Looking at the urban landscape in front of us, I slowly nodded. "And what about the ones who seem to believe that they have no control on their life and their conditions? Would you say that they're stuck in the same pattern?"

"Again, this would be a great example," Jack replied. "Everything you want in life—whether it's wealth, freedom, love, friendship, or anything else—you can have it if you take on a winner's mindset and you go get it. I'm not saying that it won't take time and effort, but if you really want it, if you believe in it, and if you do what it takes to get it, you *will* eventually have it."

"So, what is this? The power of positive thinking?" I asked, half-serious.

"I'm not asking you to take my word for it," he quickly added. "Just listen to what I have to say before you make up your mind. I truly believe that keeping a positive and optimistic mindset can serve you well in many different ways. In fact, it goes without saying that when you start thinking differently, you start acting differently as well.

"For instance, you'll start meeting new people, or seeking advice from the ones you would've normally ignored. We've talked about how important surrounding yourself with the right people was; how their attitude could either help you grow or pull you down. Well, if the people around you play such a key role in your life, imagine what your own thoughts can do."

Jack paused as we glared at each other. "A positive mindset will give you confidence. Not only that, but it will inspire you to put in the extra time and effort you need to succeed. The list goes on and on. And these are the little things that really have the power to make a difference in your life. So yes, I would call this the power of positive thinking."

In a few sentences, Jack had made his point very clear. He had also managed to effectively destroy any objection that could've crossed my mind. His explanation made perfect sense.

"How many times have I heard people say things like 'Oh, but that guy just got lucky...'" he continued. "Like it's so hard to conceive that someone can succeed by putting in the time and effort. Well, the truth is that success actually has very little to do with luck. Like I said, it's a mind game—it's about determination, positivity, and focus; not about luck."

"And how would you define a winner's mindset?"

Jack frowned. "The way I see it, having a winner's mindset is being able to stay aligned with your initial vision no matter what. In other words, it's the ability to focus on the things that matter regardless of what's trying to stand between you and your goals.

"Because you know, there are certain things that you can control in life, and others that you simply can't. It's your responsibility to choose what you focus on. For instance, you can either decide to let your past haunt you, or you can focus on what matters and plan what you're going to do next in order to achieve your goal. Needless to say, this is a critical decision."

I nodded, urging him to keep going.

"At some point in your journey to success, you will have to face certain distractions," added Jack. "Just be careful; that's when you need to stay focused. Anything that steers your attention away from your main goal is a distraction—even challenges can sometimes be distracting. If it's not going to help you move forward, don't let it bother you. That would be my advice."

"It's pretty hard to argue with that," I said, thinking out loud. "Speaking of distractions, I was just reading about Sam Walton last week when I came across something he said that really got me thinking. He was talking about how people tend to make excuses for themselves, even up to a point where they practically forget about their dreams. So, would you agree on the fact that excuses can sometimes grow into distractions?"

I had made my point clear, but it took him a moment to settle on an answer.

"I see where you're coming from," finally said Jack. "It's true that excuses will most definitely not help you move forward, and thus, you'd be right to perceive them as distractions. However, I think excuses are something else; something you need to address in a very different way.

"The way I see it, most distractions can simply be ignored or dealt with in a relatively short amount of time. Worst case scenario, they'll slow you down for a little while. But excuses are a bit different; they're just downright toxic for your growth. They have to go.

"Ask every successful man and woman out there; if you're serious about making your dreams come true, you cannot allow some B.S. excuses to paralyze you." He paused for a second and looked at me. "That said, I'm glad you brought up Sam Walton."

The sudden change in his tone caught me off guard. "Really? And why is that?"

"Because from what I've heard about the man, it seems like he never would've let the mere shadow of an excuse interfere with his ambitions. When he wanted something, he would just get up and go get it. No one was less afraid of failure than this man. That's how he built Walmart.

"When something wasn't working properly, or even when everything was fine, Walton would spend entire days in his competitors' stores," added Jack. "That's what he was known for. The guy would literally spend more time looking at the displays, touching, and measuring everything he could find in those stores than he would in his own.

"Why? Because he wanted to be ahead. He wanted Walmart to succeed. And in order for this to happen, Walton knew he had to figure out a way to make his stores better. The man had a vision, he wanted to build a retail empire, so he went out there and did just that. Some people choose to make excuses; he chose to make things happen."

"And as far as I can tell, it worked pretty well," I noted with amusement. Although I was well aware of Sam Walton's story, I never got tired of hearing it.

"At least it worked well enough to make him one of the wealthiest men on the planet—if not *the* wealthiest—by the time he died!" said Jack. "You know, he didn't *have* to do any of this; no one forced him to.

"He didn't *have* to crawl on the floor of his competitors' stores to measure the width of every aisle in case he had missed something when configuring his own stores. He didn't *have* to spend most of his time studying how others were doing business—I mean, the man was already richer than most of us will ever be! He did it because he cared. He had a vision, and every atom of his body was committed to one thing; turning it into a reality."

Again, it all made perfect sense, but I felt like a piece of the puzzle was still missing... Jack's eyes seemed lost in the urban landscape, so I stood up to face him.

"And what about those excuses?" I asked. "How do you spot them?"

"That's a good question. Here's a little context: like I said, I believe we were all born with the same opportunity in life, which is the opportunity to create the life we want to live in. So why is it that so many of us are still living a life they don't like, as if they were stuck with it?"

I sighed, my shoulders sagging. "I have no idea... I mean, I sometimes feel like this myself..."

"Then, you might want to listen carefully," Jack immediately said. "Most of these people can actually be sorted in three main categories. Some of them are already working on their dreams and are simply not quite there yet, which is fine. Others have tried and failed a few times, giving up after a handful of unsuccessful attempts.

"But what never ceases to amaze me is the following; of all the people who are stuck living a life they don't like, most simply aren't aware that they have the power to change things, which puts them in the third category. They just don't know. Can you believe that?"

"Like we're all meant to be captive of our own lives forever..." I thought out loud.

"Exactly. And although some progress has been made in the recent years to ensure that the younger generation would have a better understanding of these concepts, most schools just aren't there yet. This *has* to change. Now, if you're aware of your power to change things and you choose not to act on it, that's another story. That's when you know you're making excuses."

I nodded.

"How many times have we heard people blaming the economy for having poor sales in their business," he continued. "Sure, a recession probably will slow things down a little. But even in tough times, people still wake up every morning, drink their cup of coffee, sit in traffic for two hours, complain about their boss during the day and go to bed every night.

"The point being; life doesn't stop because the economy is in bad shape. And where there's life, there's business to be made. Believe me; if you're hungry enough, you'll find a way to make it happen. The victim mindset has to go."

"True that. I don't think I've ever heard of anyone succeeding with a victim mentality—not that I'm in a position to give advice on what it takes to succeed or anything…"

"No, you're right," said Jack. "We were born with the ability to do great things, and it's our job to acknowledge that power."

Before I could say anything, he looked at me with a compassionate smile and went on.

"You know, examples like this one are all over the place, all the time. We live in a world where most people want to have it all, but very few are actually willing to deserve it all. As a result, if you ask random people on the street what they've done today to get closer to their dreams, you're more likely to hear an excuse than a real answer."

"Like the infamous '*I don't have time…*' or '*Now is not the right time…*'" I noted.

"Especially, yes." I could feel the outrage starting to build in his voice. "I mean, how can you possibly be so busy that you don't have time to work on your dreams? This one just blows me away... If the U.S. President can fit his crazy schedule in the same 24 hours that you and I have, don't you think the real issue here might be your time management strategy?"

"If time management strategy there is," I said in an attempt to lighten the mood.

The comment made Jack chuckle. "Of course. And by the way, who said you had to wait for the 'right time' to start working on your dreams? If you can't find the right circumstances, create them. It's as simple as that. Now will always be the best time to get started."

"I think there's an old saying for that, something like—"

"The best time to plant a tree was 40 years ago; and the second best time is today," said Jack, finishing my thought. "That's right. People look at the final result and see a tree, but very few actually realize that it all starts with a seed and a little bit of faith. You'll never succeed if you keep making excuses not to move forward. All it takes is one step in the right direction."

He paused and looked at me straight in the eyes. "So tell me; what is it that's preventing you from going all in? Perhaps you don't know where to start? Fine; just get going! Believe me, you'll figure out the rest soon enough, no need to worry about that.

"You know, successful people usually don't wait for things to happen; they focus on the things they can control and get shit done. No matter what the excuse is, no matter what's holding you back, it's your responsibility to take control of your life and do something about it."

I sighed. "I know, but sometimes I feel like it's a lot easier said than done…"

"That's because you haven't found the real issue yet. It could be as simple as you not being overly comfortable with the unknown. In any case, all you need to do is to take a second to stop and analyze the situation. Think about when you first learned how to drive, or when you went to school for the first time, or when you kissed your first crush.

"You wouldn't believe how many things you've done for the first time in your life. Working on your dreams is just another one to add to the list. You don't have the skills you need? No big deal; you can always acquire them later. Here's what you need to understand; there is nothing to stop you from achieving your goals like your own mind."

I nodded. His last sentence echoed in my head for a brief moment.

"Maybe you've heard about this already," added Jack. "But Henry Ford was never really good in school. In fact, he could barely even write. But at a very young age, the boy started to grow a fascination for mechanisms. And sure enough, he became really good with them.

"As a result, Ford eventually became one of the most influential industrials of all time; one that we still remember today, even decades after his death. I guess what I'm trying to say here is that he could've simply let his weaknesses dictate his future. But instead, he chose to focus on his strengths, and leveraged them to build a legacy."

"He didn't let some pointless excuses get in the way," I said.

Jack smiled. "The man who chases two rabbits catches none, once said Confucius. Well, this also means you can't focus on your excuses and your goals all at once; it's either one or the other. You can't have both—and trust me, you don't want to be stuck with excuses."

We both remained silent for several minutes, thinking about everything that had been said in the past half hour. Once again, I had learned a lot.

After a while, Jack looked at me and finally said something. "There's a reason why I brought you here." With a subtle hand gesture, he encouraged me to come and join him. "Here, sit down and take a look in front of you."

He was pointing at the beautiful urban panorama in front of us.

"We all need somewhere we can go when our battery needs to be recharged," started Jack as I was sitting down. "And this place, this scenery; this is where I like to come when I need to have a little one-on-one chat with myself. It fuels my creativity, it inspires me; I love it here.

"So, I want you to promise me something. Promise me that you'll find a place like this for yourself; somewhere you can go to think and meditate when you feel like your motivation is fading away. Of all the things you can do to help maintain a healthy mindset, this is arguably one of the most important."

I slowly nodded. "I'll give it a serious thought. I promise."

With that, I grabbed my phone and typed a few words down to make sure I wouldn't forget my promise—something Jack seemed to appreciate.

CHAPTER 11

As much as I appreciated the view up there, I needed to move. My mind was spinning with new ideas, and I was eager to put those new lessons in action once and for all. It was time to go for a quick walk around the park.

But hardly a few minutes after we had left the bench, something in one of the trees lined up in front of us caught Jack's attention, causing him to suddenly stop walking. Slowly, the man raised his finger and pointed at what appeared to be a tiny bird nest attached to a branch.

"You're interested in birds now?" I joked, not sure of the reaction he was expecting.

It didn't seem to bother him. "There," he replied, still pointing. "You see the three babies?"

"Hmm, yeah... I guess."

"It looks like they're about to take their first flight," added Jack with a smile. "This is perfect!"

Perfect for what?

"I don't think I'm following you..." I said, confused.

"The timing couldn't have been better. These little birds are the perfect example to illustrate my next point. Any idea of what it might be?" he asked, obviously amused.

"Not really... But I feel like you're about to tell me."

"Alright. First, let me ask you this; when was the last time you did something for the first time? When was the last time you took a little run out of your comfort zone?"

I thought about it for a moment, but I couldn't tell. Clearly not expecting me to answer, Jack simply nodded and continued.

"Don't worry, most people can't tell either. The thing is; I've never heard of anyone becoming successful within the limits of their comfort zone. That's a fact."

"Yeah, I've heard about it. One of my teachers in high school used to talk about this 'comfort zone' thing to motivate his students. Frankly though, I've never really understood why everyone seems to be talking about it in a negative way."

"Trust me, you'll find out soon enough," said Jack. "If your comfort zone is providing you with all the freedom and happiness that you've ever dreamed of, then you might want to hold on to that for a while. After all, isn't this the very definition of a fulfilled life?"

I nodded. "Sure."

"Well unfortunately, comfort zone and freedom are two concepts that usually don't go all that well together. In fact, the former is mostly known for using your fears against you to prevent you from taking on new challenges and finding fulfillment. If that rings a bell, it's probably a sign that you should get out of there as soon as possible—run while you still can."

"But that's the part I don't get," I suddenly noted. "Why is it so critical?"

Jack looked away at the nest. "Because the longer you wait and you stay in that so-called comfort zone, the more afraid you'll be of leaving it. It's a vicious cycle."

Seeing the puzzled look on my face, he went on with an actual example.

"Tell me; does it seem natural for an animal—a conscious creature—to jump off a tree and expect everything to turn out fine? Of course not. And yet, some species aren't afraid to take that leap of faith. Look at these birds, for example." He pointed at the nest. "Sooner or later, they're going to have to jump out of their comfort zone to learn how to fly."

"But isn't it part of their instinct?" I interrupted him.

"Exactly. Flying is intuitive for birds; just like hunting and tracking preys is part of the cougar's genes. Birds are meant to fly; their body is designed to serve this purpose. Choosing not to do so would be fatal for them, as they would be left behind in the migration season—and eventually killed by predators. But birds intuitively know all that. That's why they do it; that's why they're not afraid to take that first jump.

"Now, what most people don't realize is that the same is also true for humans. Just like flying is part of the bird's destiny, it's part of our mission, as humans, to create a life we enjoy and to work on making our dreams come true. The reason we often don't is because we seem to have lost our ability to rely on our instincts."

I looked at him, confused. "How is that even possible?"

"Frankly, I have no idea," Jack replied. "My guess would be that it has something to do with the information overload we live in, but that's another story. One thing's for sure, it would be in everyone's best interest to recover this ability *asap*." He paused briefly. "Have you ever heard of Maslow's Hierarchy of Needs?"

"Not that I can remember, no."

"You might have heard of it as Maslow's Pyramid—that's how most people like to call it these days. Regardless, Maslow was an American psychologist mostly known for his theory on how our mental health can be influenced by the way we prioritize our basic human needs. Along with his theory, the man also came up with a structure—a pyramidal structure—to organize what he considered to be the five basic needs of humans in order of importance."

Jack reached into the inside pocket of his jacket and handed me his phone.

"Open Google and search for 'Maslow's Pyramid,'" he said. "I'll show you something."

A selection of colorful pyramid schemes appeared on the screen. "Is that it?"

"That should do it." He pointed at an image in particular. "As you can see, the bottom of the chart represents what we call the physiological needs, hence breathing, eating, sleeping, and so forth. Up one level, you have the need for safety. Of course, the need for love and belonging is the one that comes right after; everything from friendship to sexual intimacy. Then, on the fourth level of the chart, that's where you'll find the need for self-esteem and respect."

"And what about that fifth level?" I asked, intrigued. "That self-actualization thing; what's that supposed to mean?"

"Well, that's the interesting part," said Jack. "According to Maslow, the fifth and final pillar of human needs lies in self-actualization. In other words, you need problems to solve in order to find fulfillment; you need to be able to use your creativity every once in a while.

"Fulfillment is what happens when all these needs are taken care of, as a whole.

Forget one and everything goes to shit. Think about it this way; you wouldn't build a house without proper foundations or without a roof, would you? Well, that's the exact same thing. You cannot expect to live a happy and fulfilled life unless all five of your basic human needs are taken care of."

"And let me guess," I thought out loud, "this is where your comfort zone gets in the way..."

He seemed impressed. "Exactly. Because while you may be able to fulfill the first four needs of Maslow's theory within the limits of your comfort zone, I can promise you one thing; you'll never be able to do the same with your need for self-actualization."

"Then why is it that so many people spend their whole life in their comfort zone?"

"To answer that question, I think you need to look at the bigger picture," Jack replied. "While it is true that your comfort zone may limit you in various ways, I believe it can also contribute to your well-being. I mean, it does provide you with all the latitude you need to fulfill and strengthen the first few levels in your own Hierarchy of Needs. And, thereby, it allows you to build a solid foundation for the fifth and last pillar; the self-actualization part.

"Now, a lot of people dream of that day when they're just going to be set in their comfort zone forever, relaxing and doing nothing. What they don't realize is that in the long run, this cannot be a sustainable option. Because in order to be happy, you need to be challenged.

"So technically, I guess your comfort zone does have its benefits. It's a place you can go to catch your breath and make sure you're still headed in the right direction. However, I think the mistake people make here is to misinterpret this place as their final destination."

I nodded. "Alright, so when you feel like you're ready to take on new challenges, that's a sign you should probably hit the road again. Is that what you're saying?"

"Essentially, yes," said Jack. "On paper, that's pretty simple. But in reality, that's when it gets a little trickier. Like I said, the longer you stay in your comfort zone, the more afraid you'll be of going back to the real world."

Chapter 11

"Meaning what exactly?" I asked, still looking at him.

"Meaning that the end of your comfort zone also represents the beginning of your fears. That said, the only way to take full control of your mind is to face your fears. You need to make sure that you're motivated by the desire to win rather than the fear of losing."

He held his finger up to me. "You should never be afraid of trying new things every once in a while; after all, isn't it what self-actualization is all about? Don't be afraid to step off the beaten path. Just dare to take on new challenges; the opportunity to learn alone is worth a shot."

"You mean like getting involved in a new project?"

"I was thinking more about simple choices you can make on a daily basis, like taking a new route to work or trying a new restaurant. But yeah, I guess getting involved in a new project or volunteering for a cause you believe in would work too. These are all great examples of things you can do to ease your way out of your comfort zone."

Once again, I nodded my understanding.

"It's fairly simple," Jack continued. "The less power you grant to your fears, the easier it will be for you to get out of your comfort zone. Whatever you do, never let your fears impede you from finding fulfillment."

We glared at each other.

"So tell me," he began, "when was the last time you did something for the first time? I know it's actually the second time I'm asking you this, but when was the last time you dared to change something—even the slightest thing—in your daily routine? Next time someone asks you this question, you should be able to respond with a proper answer."

"I think I've heard this before," I said with a smile. "I will."

"If change used to make you uncomfortable, then maybe it's a sign you should start getting comfortable with the uncomfortable, my friend. Thomas Jefferson once said something along the lines of '*If you want something you've never had, you must be willing to do something you've never done.*'

"I don't know about you, but that makes a whole lot of sense to me. If you want what very few people have, then you've got to be willing to do what very few people do."

Chapter 11

Jack was right, it all made perfect sense. *You cannot expect to live a happy and fulfilled life unless all five of your basic human needs are taken care of.* In silence, I gave him his phone back and we both regained the trail to resume our late morning hike.

CHAPTER 12

At a distance, a young couple was playing frisbee alongside what appeared to be an artificial lake, while two ladies were sailing the water in a yellow paddleboat. Jack and I were still walking at a constant pace, and neither of us had said a word in the past five minutes.

A few steps away, a woman and her two children were lying on a plaid picnic blanket, resting under the sun. The view was absolutely gorgeous; it could've been taken directly out of a movie.

"So, what do you think would be the first step in learning how to master the unknown?" Jack began. "Anything in particular?"

"I'd say the only way to do so would be to get started somewhere; to take action."

Judging by the look on his face, he seemed to approve. "That's right. Now, of course there's always a certain risk factor you need to take into consideration before going all in into something new—but whether you succeed at it or not, at least you'll get some results."

"But what about bad results?" I said, unable to hide my concern. "You said it yourself; the only thing you can be certain of when taking action is that you're going to get results one way or the other. It's one thing if you succeed, but you could also fail..."

"So what if you fail? We've talked about this already; in each 'failure' you'll find an opportunity to learn and grow. All you have to do is learn from your mistakes and move on. No big deal."

I quickly nodded. "Right. I tend to forget about that... I'll get used to it."

"No doubt you will," answered Jack. "But, for now, what you need to remember is that action leads to results—and inaction, on the other hand, leads to dissatisfaction."

I could see the verve in his gaze as he was saying these words. "Who said you had to attain perfection on your first attempt? If every time you get involved in a new project you're under the impression that everything has to be perfect, chances are that you'll be disappointed. There's a difference between having ambitions and dwelling on desperate hopes."

"So, what do you suggest?"

Jack looked at me. "Just do your best. The outcome doesn't have to be perfect, as long as you've done your best and you know it. Not everything you do has to be flawless for it to be acceptable. You need to get rid of that misconception."

I acknowledged with a brief smile and he continued.

"Now, this whole process of getting out of your comfort zone and taking on new challenges may sound a bit counterintuitive at first, I'll give you that. But in some instances, an event could trigger the process for you, leaving you with no other option. It could be a promotion at work, a relationship status change, an accident; really anything that involves strong emotions.

"I guess what I'm trying to say here is that sometimes, circumstances can force you to take a step back from your life and look at the bigger picture. And when you do, that's when all of this usually starts to make a lot more sense."

He paused, obviously expecting some feedback.

"Well, as much as I think you're probably right about that, let's be honest here; don't you think it sounds a bit pessimistic?" I finally said. "I mean, sure, certain events can trigger a need for change, I get that. But does it have to be a tragedy? Couldn't it be an opportunity, for example?"

"Absolutely!" answered Jack in a chuckle. "If the person knows how to take advantage of the situation, I don't really see why not."

I nodded. About two hundred feet in front of us, we were able to distinguish the parking lot between the trees. It was time to go.

"I'm starving," Jack suddenly called. "Let's get out of here; lunch is on me!"

The enthusiasm in his voice made me smile. "Sounds like a plan."

"Good," he replied, looking away. "Oh, and one last thing; can you remember what I told you when we talked about excuses?"

"Sure, what about it?"

"Well, since you've had a little bit of time to get familiar with the idea, I feel like now would be a good time to give up on them once and for all. Like I said, the best thing you can do when taking action is to embrace the fact that mistakes are essential to your growth—"

"Which therefore makes excuses completely irrelevant," I interrupted him. "Got it."

"Exactly. You don't know where to start? Just do something; get out of your comfort zone and start something new. No matter what it is, just get started somewhere and let everything else fall into place. You wouldn't believe all the things you can accomplish. You just need to get started."

One thing I really liked about Jack was his ability to find the right words to resonate with my teenage mind. Again, the man had me feeling like I was sitting on top of the world, ready to take on any challenges that life would throw at me.

Back in the parking lot, four college boys were gathered around the bright red Ferrari, taking pictures of the car. Seeing that, Jack looked at me and tossed me the keys.

"Be careful," he said. "I really love that car."

It took me a few seconds to realize that he wasn't kidding. I couldn't believe it. For as long as I could remember, I had always dreamt of being able to drive one of those cars. My excitement was undeniable. Without waiting, I rushed to the driver's side and sat behind the wheel, letting the dream take a whole new dimension.

In the palm of my hands, I could feel the soft grain of the Italian leather covering the steering wheel. The smell, the colors, the brutal sound coming from the engine bay; everything was just so perfect. I was living the dream of every car enthusiast my age. And thanks to what my mentor had taught me, I was able to make the most of every second of it. What a blessing.

CHAPTER 13

We had been sitting in traffic for a few minutes at most, and already, I couldn't believe how much of an attention magnet this car was. People pointing at it and smiling, kids turning heads at the sound of the roaring engine; we had seen it all. Somehow, it made me realize how much of a positive impact Jack had had in my life so far.

In an attempt to avoid Montreal's lunchtime rush hour, I jumped on the closest highway. We were now heading west on the Trans-Canada Highway, and I had no idea where Jack wanted me to go. When I looked at him for directions, he seemed just as confused as I was.

"Barbie's?" he finally said, pointing at a sign on the side of the road.

The name instantly revived old memories. "Sure," I replied. "I haven't been there in years!"

Jack nodded.

I felt like a little kid behind the wheel of the 458 Italia. To my surprise, the ride quality was actually quite impressive—nowhere near what I would've expected from a car with such a low ground clearance. *No wonder people call this a gentleman's car.*

When we pulled in the parking lot of the restaurant, most heads turned in our direction once again. Although I had never been a huge fan of flashy things, I remember thinking that I could definitely get used to this one.

As soon as we walked in, a waitress assigned us to a table and handed us two menus.

"Have you ever tried to find your purpose?" Jack suddenly asked, glancing at the menu.

"My purpose?" I slowly answered.

Seeing the puzzled look on my face, he closed his menu and said, "I'm talking about your inner calling; your motivation to get out of bed every morning and crush your goals."

"Oh... I don't think so, no."

"Good. Then let's do it right now."

Chapter 13

I nodded my approval in silence, and Jack continued.

"Over the years, as I've had the chance to discuss with many successful people, I've come to discover that most of them had something in common; they all have a defined life purpose. Ask each and everyone of them, they all know exactly why they're doing what they do.

"Believe it or not, I think that's one of the main reasons they're doing so well. Why? Because having a purpose helps you stay on top of your game; it helps you stay consistent. Simply put, a purpose is like a very strong, deep-rooted source of motivation. And since you need motivation to stay consistent, I think having a purpose can come in pretty handy."

"And what about you?" I asked. "When did you find yours?"

"I found mine over a decade ago," Jack answered, apparently expecting the question. "Some people like to pretend they don't have one; others think they simply don't need one. But in my opinion, you've got to have a purpose. It goes just without saying."

I looked at him, confused. "See, that part I don't get... I mean, I've had a pretty decent life so far, and yet I wasn't even aware of all this. So, how do you explain that?"

"Well, let's not forget; you're 17. And of course, not having a purpose doesn't mean you can't live a decent life! Will you be able to find fulfillment and ultimate happiness? I don't think so. If this is what you're looking for, then you have to find your life purpose."

"And what if you can't find it?"

The question made him smile. "Then you need to keep looking. Because the truth is, we all have one. Somewhere, deep down, we all have a purpose. Now, it is our job to narrow it down and define it properly for ourselves, but rest assured, we all have one."

"If what you're saying is true, then the people who pretend that they can't find theirs are no different than those who never take action; they're just making excuses..."

"Sounds like you don't even need me anymore!" said Jack, holding a laugh. "You're right. And this can only mean one thing; finding your purpose is just like anything else. If this is what you want, you've got to be willing to deploy your efforts in that direction and go get it."

I nodded. "You mentioned earlier that most successful people you know used their purpose to help maintain a certain level of consistency. But what about those who never actually take the time to sit down and think about their inner calling? What happens with them?"

"Good question. From what I've seen, most of them will spend the rest of their lives fighting a nagging felling of emptiness. Others will simply end up giving up on their dreams as soon as they're given a chance, when the road in front of them gets a little bumpy."

"That's pretty sad…"

"Maybe, but remember; no one's going to do the work for you. If you decide to go down that road and to give up on your dreams, well, you're the only one to be held accountable for your choice. We were all born with the same opportunity in life—"

"The opportunity to decide," I said, finishing his thought.

"Exactly. So at the end of the day, it's your call to make. Now, the good news is that no matter how old you get, you can always go back and find your purpose. Of course, the sooner you find it, the better. But it's never too late to have that conversation with yourself."

I looked at him, surprised. "Really?"

"Really," said Jack with a nod. "So, what's the meaning you want to give to your life? I know this is getting deep, but you need to ask yourself; what's the point of getting up every morning and going to work if you have no idea *why* you're doing all of that?"

I remained silent. We were glaring at each other.

"When the challenges arise," he added, "who would you rather be; the one who gives up and loses or the one who fights and wins?"

"The winner," I said in a confident tone.

"Then you need to have a vision. And having a purpose is part of having a good vision."

Again, I nodded my understanding.

"Mark Twain once said that the two most important days in a man's life are the day he's born and the day he finds out why," Jack continued. "I guess that's a pretty accurate way to illustrate just how important a purpose can be in someone's life, don't you think?"

As he pronounced these words, the waitress stopped by our table to take our orders. Jack went for a smoked meat sandwich and a Coke, while I asked for the cheeseburger and a glass of water. It looked so delicious on the menu, I just couldn't resist. I was starving.

"It's a fundamental value," said Jack after the waitress had left with the two menus. "No one invented this; living with a purpose is just how things have shown to work out best."

"I get it, but—"

"How do you find it?" he interrupted me, smiling.

I laughed. "Well, it all sounds good on paper, I agree, but how do you find it? I mean, how can you know without a doubt that whatever you find is your life purpose and not something else? How—"

"Whoa! Slow down, man! One question at a time."

"I got carried away... Sorry, I'm listening."

Amused, Jack approached slightly and rested his forearms on the edge of the table. "Let's try to reverse-engineer this for a second. First of all, do you think it's possible to see if a person has found their purpose? And if so, how?"

I thought about it for a moment. "I have no idea."

"Passion," Jack promptly added. "You'll know they've found their 'why'—their purpose—when all you can see in their eyes is a burning passion for what they do. It's pretty hard to miss; just being alive seems to be a true blessing to them. People with a clear purpose are usually very passionate about life. That's how you'll know.

"Does this mean everything always goes exactly as planned for them? Probably not. But the truth is, most of them don't even care about things going according to plan. Why? Because they gave their life a meaning; they have a vision. They *know* it's just a matter of time before they get where they want to be."

He looked me in the eyes. "As a result, you'll notice that people with a purpose tend to enjoy their life a lot more than others typically would, mainly because they're not spending all their time and energy worrying about every detail."

"Makes sense," I muttered as I began to connect the dots in my head. "That passion you're talking about, I can see it in your eyes. It's pretty obvious that you love what you do. Clearly, you seem to enjoy sharing your knowledge like that, which I think is admirable, by the way.

"You know, up until now, I had never really understood why you'd go out of your way to help me like you did. I mean, I've always been grateful for it, don't get me wrong. But ever since we met for the first time in that car accident, I've always wondered why you did what you did. And today I think I've found my answer; you're simply living your purpose."

"There you go," Jack slowly said, still looking at me. "Knowing that, let me ask you; what's the first step you would take to find yours?"

"I think the first thing I would do would be to figure out what my main passion is."

"Interesting. That's a good start. Now, when you're looking for answers, what do you normally do? You ask questions. And finding your purpose is no exception; asking yourself a bunch of questions is probably the best way to ignite the whole process."

I frowned. "And what kind of questions are we talking about exactly?"

"Well, it depends," he replied, slightly raising his hands. "The whole idea is to get to know yourself a little better. Therefore, I would personally try to focus on my passions and interests to begin with—but that's just me. Does it mean it's the only way to go? Definitely not. But if you ask me, that's the first place I would start looking.

"Just find out what you really love; something you really care about. From there, everything's just going to fall into place. It could be a cause, a leisure; as long as it's something that makes you happy, something you're genuinely passionate about. That would be the first step."

"Okay, so if I wanted to get started right now, what exactly would you suggest—"

"Actually, you know what?" Jack suddenly asked, interrupting me. "I have a better idea. Let's do this together; let's go through the whole process together."

With a smile, I raised both my hands in surrender and let him take the lead.

"Alright. So like I said, the first step would be to ask yourself a bunch of questions in order to figure out what your main passion is. And be careful here; something you just like doing every once in a while isn't going to cut it. You need to pick something you're really passionate about."

"Well, to be honest, I'd say personal development has been growing on me lately. I know it's still fairly new to me, but I feel like the more I read about it—and the more we talk about it—the more I want to know about it."

Jack nodded. "Sounds good. Now, think about this for a second; if you had all the money in the world, what would you do? How would you spend your days in a meaningful way?"

He emphasized on "meaningful."

"Honestly, I think I would travel the world and attend seminars on all sorts of things. I feel like that's something I'd really like to do."

"That's it?" Jack replied, apparently expecting a little more.

"Hmm, I would probably start a nonprofit to help those in need. And with any time left, I would read and expand my knowledge on various subjects; maybe even attend a cooking class. Other than that, I don't really know what to say..."

"But you get the idea, right?" He looked at me. "If you want to find your purpose, you need to be able to answer these questions. Now, of course finding your passion is a significant step in the right direction, but it doesn't end there.

"Passion alone is only going to take you so far. I mean, sure, it's an asset you can use to help stay motivated, but it's not going to do the work for you. In other words, I guess you could think of it more as a map; it's going to show you the road, but it won't take you to your destination."

"Then what's the missing part?" I asked, eager to hear the answer.

"To find your purpose, you'll need to acknowledge your personal strengths. We were all born with a talent—or a special gift, as I like to call it. Believe it or not, we're all gifted with a special ability; we're all good at something, but it's our job to acknowledge it. Because we all know what we're good at, but very few of us are willing to admit it. So, any clue what it might be for you?"

"Well, I'm pretty good at writing... But to be honest, I don't really see how this has anything to do with my purpose..."

Before I could finish, Jack lifted his finger to interrupt me. "Here's the thing," he said. "When you're passionate about something, you're more likely to be good at it. Because the truth is, our passions and our strengths tend to be very closely related.

"Of course, it's not an exact science; meaning that your talent and your main passion could also be completely unrelated. But, in any case, you want to make sure that you leave no stone unturned.

"For example, if you're passionate about the human body and your talent lies in your ability to use science like no one else, then maybe your purpose is to find a cure for cancer. If you know everything there is to know about baseball and you also happen to be a good writer, then maybe you were born to write about it, making sure that the legends are never forgotten."

In silence, I nodded my understanding.

"With that, you should already have a better idea of what you're looking for," he added. "And if not, don't worry; maybe you just haven't found your real passion yet. Either way, your purpose will reveal itself at some point down the road, when you're ready and you're moving in the right direction. Just make sure you keep an eye open for it."

"Focus on the things you can control and stop worrying about the rest," I said with a smile.

The reference made him chuckle. "Exactly. Now, once you've found your special gift, it's time to start fine-tuning it. That's where the real work begins. Because no matter what it is that you're trying to do, you want to have an edge; you want to be able to stand out from the crowd."

"But don't you think that the simple fact of being aware of your talent automatically makes you stand out?" I asked. "I mean, that sounds like an edge to me..."

"In a certain way, I guess it does. But it's never going to be nearly enough to guarantee you any kind of success. Take hockey players for example; there's probably over five million of them in Canada alone. And among these five million, how many make it to the NHL?"

"Six or seven hundred, maybe? I don't know…"

"Well, one thing's for sure; all five million of them are probably better than me with a hockey stick and a puck," Jack continued. "What I'm trying to say is that being aware of your strengths is a good start; it's just not enough to make you stand out.

"If you want to play with the big boys, you need to work on your skills. You need to pick one thing you're really good at, and learn how to master it. Because when everyone else around you is good, being good isn't going to cut it. You have to be great. It's as simple as that."

"And what about our weaknesses? I mean, if we all have our strengths, it also implies that we have our weaknesses. So, how do you deal with those?"

"Good question," he answered, looking at me. "Opinions tend to vary about that. Some will say that you should work hard on improving them, but I beg to differ. To me, the best way to handle this would be to leave your flaws alone and focus on your strengths."

I laughed. "Pretty straightforward. And why is that?"

"Because working on your weaknesses will only make you average at best, whereas working on your strengths will make you great. That's how you'll stand out. Now, once you feel confident enough with your craft, all you have to do is to start building your team; a team made of people whose skill sets match your shortcomings. And there you go."

"Leveraging everyone's individual strengths to create one big winning team. I love the idea!"

As I was saying this, the waitress arrived with our drinks and our meals. My cheeseburger looked delicious.

"Maybe you were born to be one of the greatest hockey players of all time and show people that anything is possible," Jack said as the waitress walked away. "Or maybe you were born to find a cure for cancer; there's no good or bad answer here. Whatever your purpose may be, we were all born to achieve greatness in our own way."

CHAPTER 14

As soon as my alarm went off, I jumped in the shower and rushed downstairs to grab a quick bite on the go. Two weeks had gone by since my last meeting with Jack, and today was the day we were supposed to pick up where we had left off. I couldn't have been more excited.

We had agreed to meet at his office later in the morning, which gave me just enough time to get ready and drive there. When I finally entered the building, Jack's assistant kindly walked me to his office down the hallway. That's where I found him, squeezing a stress reliever.

"How've you been, buddy?" Jack exclaimed as soon as he saw me.

"Doing great!" I replied, shaking his hand. "Nice to see you."

"You too. So, what's up?"

"Actually, I've been thinking a lot about our last meeting over the past few days, and I think I might be onto something."

He smiled. "I'm listening."

"I think I've found my purpose—at least for now. I think I was born to use my writing skills to help people my age find their way and leave their mark in this world."

"Interesting. And how exactly are you going to achieve this? What are you planning on doing to make it happen?" he asked, obviously challenging me.

I looked at him in disbelief. "Well, that's another story..."

"Alright. Come over here; have a seat."

Jack pointed to one of the two armchairs facing his desk and continued.

"You need to have a plan; we've talked about that already. No matter what your goal is, if you want to achieve it, you've got to have some sort of plan in place. Now, before you go and try to make one on your own, I have a few guidelines that I'd like to share with you."

In silence, I nodded.

"Good. So, first and foremost, before you can start managing your goals, you've got to learn how to manage yourself."

Chapter 14

Before I could even say anything, he went on to explain his thought.

"It's one thing to have a plan, but if you can't execute it properly, then you're back to square one. In order to make this work, you've got to be able to organize your actions. And I'm not just talking about having a time structure—although this could be just as important. I'm talking about deciding whether or not certain actions are worth being taken more than others.

"Take a look around you; you'll see some things that you can control, and other things that you simply cannot control. That's just how it goes; everything you can imagine in life falls into either one of these two categories.

"For example, let's say you have an important meeting downtown on a week day. Traffic and red lights are going to slow you down, but these are things that you cannot control. Something you can control, however, would be the time at which you leave. You could very well decide to leave ten minutes earlier to make sure you get there on time. You see the difference here?"

"I do," I replied with a quick nod.

"Now, being effective in the way you manage yourself means being able to focus on what you can control and let go of what's out of your power. In other words, perhaps you won't always be able to control how things unfold in your life, but one thing's for sure; you'll always be able to choose how you react to them."

"Like the weather," I said, trying to illustrate Jack's thought. "You can't control the temperature outside, but you can pick your clothes accordingly."

"Exactly. Plan for the long term, and make your actions count on the short term. Now, it also means that you've got to have some sort of structure in place in your life.

"Of course, scheduling and planning is probably the most annoying part of the process, but it's also an essential key to success. Again, it's all about consistency; about making the little steps count. Add a proper time structure to that and you're good to go."

With both hands in his pockets, Jack was now standing right in front of me.

"Next," he continued. "Learning how to manage your life also means that you're going to want to hold yourself accountable for the actions you take. The sooner you acknowledge the fact that you're responsible for both your successes and failures, the more decision power you'll have over your conditions and your life in general."

"Meaning what exactly?"

"Meaning that you're the only one responsible for making the right choices and being the best version of yourself at all times. Whatever it is that you're trying to accomplish, whether you end up succeeding or not, it's on you. You're the one in charge; you need to understand that."

I remained silent for a moment. "That sounds like a lot of pressure to me..."

"In a certain way, I guess it is. I mean, when you agree to hold yourself accountable for your choices, you also agree to live with the consequences of your thoughts and actions. Nothing particularly exciting here, you're right.

"However, being the one in charge also means that you're absolutely free to do whatever you want, whenever you want. In other words, with each new day, you have an opportunity to create the life of your dreams. And that, to me, is worth its weight in gold."

I nodded. Jack was right; ironically, it all made perfect sense.

Staring at the skyline through the window, he remained silent for a minute or two.

"Another habit I'd recommend you develop would be to make sure you always begin with the end in mind," Jack spontaneously said, grabbing his stress reliever. "Meaning that if your goal is to become a wildly successful writer, you've got to be able to visualize yourself having already achieved that, even before—"

Seeing the puzzled look on my face, he stopped mid-sentence.

"Alright, let's take this from the beginning. You've probably heard of this before, but our mind is structured in two distinct segments; the conscious part and the subconscious part. What most people seem to ignore, however, is that our subconscious acts like a gigantic database that keeps track of everything we encounter. Every line of text we read, every face we see, every song we hear; if it goes through our brain, our subconscious mind keeps track of it all."

"Really? I didn't know that..." I slowly said, unable to hide my amazement.

"We can't remember everything, because the conscious mind wouldn't be able to handle so much data. But it's all there, archived somewhere in our subconscious, which counts for about 90% of our brain.

"Now, another characteristic trait of the subconscious mind is that it never sleeps. Unlike its conscious counterpart, it doesn't need to, because it doesn't think. So, whatever information you choose to feed your mind with, your subconscious will just soak it up like a sponge, regardless of the context in which it was taken in the first place."

"Just like that?" I suddenly asked. "I mean, there's got to be a certain thought process in the way our mind stores all this information, right?"

Jack shook his head, looking at me. "Actually, no. The conscious mind uses logic, we know that, but somehow, the subconscious seems to be very literal and impartial. Therefore, you've got to be really careful what you let in there."

"And then what?" I laughed. "You're going to tell me that our brain works like a computer with unlimited capacities, maybe? Come on, man... I'm not falling for that—"

The serious look on his face caught me off guard. He really *was* going to say that.

"Exactly," said Jack as soon as I finished my little monologue. "Because that's exactly what it is; a computer that stores data and commands. Why do you think habits are so powerful?"

Before I could put another word in, he continued.

"When you're looking to change an old behavior, you basically want to convince your mind to overwrite that brain pattern. By doing things over and over again, you develop new habits, and that's how you can get rid of certain behaviors or limiting beliefs. You know that already.

"But this is where it gets interesting; with all the data it contains, it's your subconscious that drives you to make certain decisions or take certain actions more than others. Somehow, it can lead you to accomplish all sorts of things—sometimes even without you noticing.

"Now, since your subconscious mind doesn't think, it cannot differentiate what's true from what's not. So, whatever it is that you imagine, your mind will figure out a way to make it happen for you. Once you understand that, a whole new world of possibilities opens up to you, because it means you can now plant just about any idea into your mind and turn it into a reality."

That was a lot to process, especially so early in the morning.

"I can teach you how to take advantage of it if you want," Jack added with a smile, seeing the perplexed look on my face.

Doing my best to get my thoughts together, I nodded.

"Alright. So, the first thing you want to do is to set yourself a proper goal—don't worry, you'll see exactly what I mean by that a little later. But yeah, you want to start with an intention. Once you have a clear vision of your goal, you want to convince your mind that it is part of your new reality; and that's when visualization comes into play."

"Visualization?"

"That's right." He was still standing, facing me. "You need to think, but most importantly, you need to *feel* like you've already achieved your goal. You think you can do that?"

"I can try... But how do you trick your feelings like that anyway? I mean, no matter how much I try to act and think like a millionaire, it doesn't change the fact that I only have about $2000 in my name right now. How am I supposed to feel like a millionaire with that?"

"Well, there are a few things you could do to try and spark your creativity," Jack answered.

I frowned. "Like what?"

"You could start by looking online for articles on how to become financially free, maybe watch a few video interviews with millionaires and billionaires, see what they do. You want to learn as much as you can about their lifestyle; what their morning routine looks like, how much time they usually spend at work, what kind of car they drive, etc.

"And then, you want to try to implement these habits into your own life. Wake up earlier in the morning, for example. Watch less TV; go to the gym if necessary. It's going to require a little bit of discipline, but the end result should be worth it."

I nodded in silence.

Chapter 14

"Another thing you could do would be to visualize yourself in the future," he said.

"In the future?"

"Well, if you feel like it's too big of a stretch to imagine yourself being a millionaire in today's date, you can always try to picture it in four or five years from now. Maybe that's all you need to start believing in the possibility of it happening for real."

"I can see that working," I muttered, thinking out loud.

Jack smiled warmly. "Like I said, your subconscious mind can't make the difference between what's real and what's not. Meaning that if you can make yourself *feel* like a millionaire, whether it's in the present or the future, you should be able to get a similar outcome."

I pulled out my phone and noted a few keywords. "Anything else I should know?"

"Actually, yes. From my personal experience, a great way to make your visualizations even more effective would be to incorporate a lot of symbols and images in the process. Because it's not just about *seeing* what you want; it's about *experiencing* it with all your senses. The more detailed your experience is, the better your chances of getting exactly what you asked for."

"So, that's how you can start attracting what you want, eh?"

"If you're emotionally engaged in the whole process, yes," Jack replied. "Because emotions also play a very important role here. But generally speaking, if you do a good job visualizing with all your senses, emotions should emerge without you having to worry too much about them."

Unfortunately, that was precisely the issue with me. No matter how hard I tried to act and feel like a millionaire, even with all the tips Jack had given me, it didn't feel right. My conscious mind was holding me back, and that's exactly what I told him.

"No worries; I can relate," Jack responded in a comforting tone. "I've been through the same struggle a thousand times myself. It's pretty common."

"And you found a way out?"

"One of my mentors taught me this old trick when I was about your age. Although it's a fairly simple concept, I'm still using it even to this day." He paused briefly. "The idea is to be gradual in the way you approach your desires. For example, you could start by getting comfortable with the following statement: '*I am now ready to accept the fact that I'm on the right path to achieve my goal of becoming a millionaire.*'

"Once you feel good with that, you can step it up a notch and go with the following: '*I am now on the right path to achieve my goal of becoming a millionaire.*' And then, to push it another step forward, you could try: '*I am now progressively becoming a millionaire.*' Until—"

"Until you can say '*I am now a free millionaire.*' and be totally confident about it," I interrupted him, smiling. "That's pretty clever."

Jack smiled back and added, "With these statements, you're basically conditioning your mind to believe that your goal is attainable. Once you have that belief, all you need to do is just take action and let go."

"And let go?" I repeated after him.

"Hold your horses," he said in a laughter. "Letting go certainly doesn't mean giving up on all the principles we've seen so far. The way I see it, letting go is more of a way to detach yourself from potential failure—or feedback in general, should I say."

He looked at me to make sure I was paying attention. "Remember the little birds we saw the other day? They were about to jump out of their nest for the first time; to take that leap of faith and learn how to fly. Everything could've gone wrong in that first attempt, but it didn't. The birds simply followed their instincts; they jumped and let go.

"Of course, I'm oversimplifying here, but that just goes to say that if you take inspired action and believe that everything is going to be fine, it probably will. Don't let hesitation and worries hold you back; just act, and then let go. From there, what's meant to happen will happen."

Jack was right. Sometimes in life, the best thing to do is to follow your instincts, take inspired action and let go some of the things you can't control.

As soon as he noticed that I had grasped that, he went on to say:

"So yeah, all in all, that's what I'm talking about when I'm saying you should make it a habit to always begin with the end in mind."

Chapter 14

Still comfortably seated in one of the two armchairs facing Jack's desk, I nodded.

"Now, the third and last guideline I have for you is one that should really help you plan your actions more effectively," added Jack. "It's a philosophy I like to call *first things first*."

"First things first," I repeated slowly, trying to seize the hidden meaning of these words.

"It's about prioritizing what's important to you versus of what's considered urgent by everyone else's standards."

Somehow, his answer struck me by surprise. "But how can there be anything more pressing than the urgent itself?"

"Because we live in a world where we tend to forget what the real emergencies are. We're so busy trying to handle all our day-to-day crises that we often end up forgetting about the things that really matter.

"Think about it for a second; what's 'urgent' for people nowadays? New friend requests? New text messages? Late night calls from grumpy clients? I don't know what happened to the world over the past decade or so, but we've totally lost it. Your number one priority should be on the things that really matter to you, not on all that stupid nonsense."

"You sure have a point there."

"To build long-term success, you've got to have the integrity to act on *your* priorities," Jack continued. "You can't remain in perfect alignment with your goals and keep answering every text message, every call and every email all at once. You just can't. To be successful, you need to give up on being busy and learn how to become effective."

As he was saying that, I looked up and saw him back to the window, staring at the skyline.

"So, what is it that I have to do?" I asked, intrigued.

"You simply need to start prioritizing what's truly important to you. You need to start building your schedule *around* the things that matter, not *in spite* of them. For example, if having dinner with your family every night is something you really care about, you should make it a priority to block time for that in your schedule.

"Meaning that when a client asks for a meeting at six o'clock on a Wednesday night,

Chapter 14

it's your responsibility to honor your other engagement and suggest a better time. I'm pretty sure that's what you would do if you had another appointment, so why can't you just do it for yourself?"

Jack definitely had a solid point there.

"You may have heard that story before," he added before I could put a word in. "It's a lesson a college teacher taught to a group of students a couple of years ago. The teacher, in front of his group, took a transparent jar and filled it with golf balls. He then looked at the students and asked them if the jar was full.

"Without thinking, everyone in the room said yes. Satisfied, the teacher grabbed the jar and poured a handful of wooden beads in it, which went to fit right in between the golf balls. He then looked at the students and asked the same question. Same answer.

"After conducting the experiment again with sand and water, the teacher sat down in front of his class and said, 'When you let the small stuff clutter up your life, it becomes much harder to make room for what's important—'"

"But when you go the other way around and you put what's important first, everything else eventually falls into place," I said, completing his thought.

"Exactly." He raised both his hands, palms facing up. "So, now that you know how to manage yourself, begin with the end in mind, and set your priorities; what do you think is next?"

CHAPTER 15

We were both having conversation in his office when Jack had suddenly grabbed the keys on his desk and urged me to follow him.

A minute later, we were out in the parking lot, walking towards his Bentley—and again, I had no idea where he had planned to take me.

"What exactly do you know about self-awareness?" asked Jack when we got to the car.

"Well, aside from what you've told me thus far, I don't know all that much. I remember you saying something about the responsibility that each and everyone of us has towards their own successes and failures, but that's pretty much all I can think of…"

He nodded. "That's a good start, but as I'm sure you can imagine, there's a lot more to it than that—we'll talk about it in a moment. But first, let me ask you this; on a scale of one to ten, how self-aware would you consider yourself?"

The question kind of caught me off guard. "That's a tough one," I mumbled in a chuckle. "I'd probably give myself a four, or maybe a five... I don't know. What about you?"

"I'd say somewhere between an eight and a nine, depending on the day. And I'm still working on it. For a 17-year-old, though, five is a pretty good number. You said you wanted to become a well-known writer; an inspiration for young people. Well, self-awareness is what's going to pave the way for you to turn that vision into a reality."

"And how is that?" I asked, perplexed.

Jack smiled, his eyes on the road. "Because in one way or another, self-awareness is at the center of everything we've talked about so far. It's the cornerstone that connects every concept and every lesson that we've seen.

"Think about it; how could you possibly think of being able to find your purpose without first getting to know yourself on a deeper level? Do you think you could learn from your mistakes? Because in order to do so, you need to be able to acknowledge them in the first place. And what about that vision you have for your dreams? It's simple; you've got to know who you are and what you want for it to be accurate.

"These are just a few examples," added Jack, still looking at the road. "If you're going to use these principles to build the life of your dreams, then you've got to understand that self-awareness is the foundation of every single one of them."

"Makes sense," I said with a quick nod.

"Having an 'awareness' mindset can help you on many levels," he continued. "For example, it allows you to make deliberate decisions and be more objective, preventing your emotions from clouding your judgement in certain situations. In other words, the more conscious you are of what's going on in your life, the more control you have over your own destiny."

"What do you mean?"

"Well, what's great about self-awareness is that it requires you to question and analyze the person you are from an inner perspective. And to be honest, I don't think there's a better way to improve than to know exactly what you're good at and what you still have to learn.

"The more you get to know yourself, the easier it becomes for you to adapt and bond with your surroundings. Why? Because you're the one in control. You know what's going on, you're aware of your capabilities, and therefore, you're in complete control of your life."

I looked at him, puzzled. "I get the idea, but how exactly does it apply to you and me?"

"Here's an example," Jack replied, apparently expecting the question to come up. "Have you ever been in a situation where you were asked to work on a project with someone and just felt like doing all the work by yourself?"

"It used to happen a lot in high school, yes."

"And why is that?"

"I don't know, maybe to get all the credit," I slowly answered. "Something like that."

"Maybe you're right. But my guess is that you simply weren't self-aware enough. Because if you were, you would've known that you can't be good at everything you do. You would've known your limitations, and you would've been in a position to leverage your partner's strengths—"

"But instead, I took the lead and never gave them a chance to show their skills," I thought out loud, interrupting him. "Makes sense."

Jack nodded quietly. "Things like that don't happen when you're in a state of awareness. And don't get me wrong; I'm sure you were able to handle the assignment just fine on your own, no question about it. I guess what I'm trying to say is that maybe your partner would've brought the extra 'wow' to your final result; the little touch that would've made it outstanding."

"In other words, being in a state of awareness puts you in a position where you can basically make the most of every situation," I calmly stated. "Is that what you're saying?"

"In a nutshell, yes. It puts you on top of your game; it gives you an edge."

"But does it end somewhere? I mean, once you know yourself inside out, you can't really dig much deeper than that, can you? So then, what's next?"

"I'm glad you asked," he promptly replied while making a left turn. "Actually, the cycle doesn't quite end there. Once you've reached a comfortable level of self-awareness and you know just about everything there is to know about yourself, you get into what I like to call a state of 'global awareness.' That's when you start being aware of what's going on *around* you."

I remained silent for a moment, waiting for him to go into details.

"Self-awareness is about understanding what sets you apart. It's about understanding what makes you who you are. How are you different from your friends and family? What talents were you born with? You've got to be able to answer these questions. Once you're done figuring that out, that's when the state of 'global awareness' kicks in; that's when you get to learn how—"

"But that's the part I don't understand," I interrupted him. "Self-awareness is important, I get what the fuss is all about. But why would I want to be aware of what's going on in other people's lives when I know for a fact that I'm the only one responsible for my own success?"

"Well, Pablo Picasso once said something along the lines of, 'Good artists copy, great artists steal.' Meaning that no matter what we do in life, we all have our influences. Some people just take an existing idea and run away with it. Others create a whole new interpretation of that idea and make it their own. The point being; we all take our ideas somewhere."

He looked at me. "That's why increasing your level of awareness towards your surroundings can come in pretty handy; because it allows you to find inspiration and new ideas more easily."

I nodded slowly.

"That said, make sure you don't let your ego get in the way."

"What do you mean?"

"You know, with all that knowledge, it's easy to get cocky and let your ego steal the show. You don't want that. Because yes, it's important to pay attention to your surroundings, but you don't want to end up losing sight of your own goals either. So, it's all about finding the right balance."

We glared at each other in silence for a second, and Jack continued.

"The perfect example of a situation like this actually happened to me about a year ago, when I left my previous company to start the business I'm currently involved in. When I announced my decision to leave, some of my fellow colleagues got a little upset, knowing that I was about to become their first real competitor.

"They became so obsessed with trying to see what I was doing on my side of the fence that they almost completely forgot about their own business. It even reached a point where I would see their general manager drive by my store three to four times a day... It was just ridiculous."

"Seriously?" I asked, unable to hide my surprise.

"Unfortunately for them, yes. Now, what do you think happened during that time? God knows how many opportunities they've missed. While they were busy trying to figure out how I'd play my cards, I was the one attending all the auctions and buying all the cars I wanted for pennies on the dollar. Needless to say, this took a pretty big hit on their business."

"And gave you the advantage," I said, completing his thought.

Jack nodded. "Exactly. So, you want to keep an eye on your surroundings, yes, but you also want to be careful not to let your ego steer you in the wrong direction.

"When you start living in a state of awareness, everything around you then becomes tinted by that vision. You start noticing things you would've normally ignored, feeling more present, and that's exactly the kind of mindset you need to start seeing all the opportunities around you.

"Who knows; the next billion-dollar idea could come to you from that weird woman you met at the restaurant the other day, or maybe from the homeless man you helped on the subway. You never know what life is going to throw at you."

CHAPTER 16

This has got to be a joke, I thought.

When I saw the fancy welcome sign by the parking lot entrance and realized where Jack was taking me, I must admit, I got a little nervous. Apparently, the man thought it would be a good idea to initiate me to the virtues of golfing. Needless to say, I wasn't expecting this; hell, I didn't even know he played golf.

"Come on," Jack said with a friendly smile as soon as he saw the look on my face. "You said you had never played before. It'll be fun."

I slowly shook my head in disbelief. "Sounds like we're going to be here for a while. Might as well try to make the most of it."

Jack smiled and we both got out of the car. Luckily, the course wasn't packed, meaning that we probably wouldn't have to worry too much about slowing down the game.

When we reached the back of the car, Jack popped the trunk to reveal his clubs—a full set of beautiful TaylorMade Burner 2.0 irons—and two pairs of Nike golf shoes. Turns out he had been planning this little stunt after all...

"We've talked about the main difference between a dream and a goal, right?" Jack asked as we entered the clubhouse.

"Yeah; you said a goal was essentially a dream with a deadline."

He nodded and paid the fare for the both of us.

"But you never told me how to actually set one," I said, walking out of the building.

"And that's exactly why I brought you here," he replied. "To show you how. Because setting a proper goal is one thing, but then you've got to be able to achieve it."

As he pronounced these words, Jack put on a white leather glove on his left hand and chose one of the irons from his bag. After taking a few warm-up swings, he looked down in silence and hit the white ball with

Chapter 16

the precision of a pro golfer. The round had officially begun.

"And for that, you're going to need a clear vision, of course, but you're also going to have to be very action-oriented," he continued, visibly quite proud of his first shot. "So, how do you take a dream and turn it into an actual goal?

"Well, for starters, you've got to decide on what it is that you're going to achieve. It could be just about anything; it doesn't really matter as long as it's something you genuinely care about."

Jack handed me his club and gave me a few directions. Doing my best to stay focused and keep my eyes on the ball, I took a first swing and missed. Instead, a piece of turf went flying above our heads, leaving me dumbfounded. On my second attempt, however, I was able to hit the ball and see it fall right in the middle of the fairway.

"Not bad for a first try," Jack said with a half-smile. "It sure doesn't look like it's your first time on a golf course..."

"I might have been to the driving range once or twice when I was a kid." I couldn't hide my amusement anymore.

We both burst out laughing.

"So, what is it that you want to achieve?" he asked as we started walking down the cart path.

I took a minute to think about it. "I'd like to have my first book written and published by the end of next year. Ambitious, but achievable."

"Alright. Now, the next step is pretty simple; write it down. I don't care if it's in your journal, on your wall or in a little notebook next to your bed, just write it down somewhere you can see it."

In silence, I nodded.

"And then," Jack continued, "you want to get out there and tell everyone about it. You want to advertise your goal; we've talked about that already, remember?"

As he said that, Jack pulled a shorter iron from the bag and set up for his second shot. At a distance, I saw the white ball fall right in the middle of the green and roll slightly to the left.

"I remember. That's why I'm telling you; my goal is to have my first book published by the end of next year."

"Fair enough," he answered. "So, how long is your typical nonfiction book? 150 to 200 pages maybe? Let's say 200. Now, what you need to do is take that goal and break it down into much smaller steps.

"One way to do it would be to find a subject, write an outline, and then start writing the actual book one chapter at a time—or even better, one single page at a time. This way, you can focus on one small task at a time, get it done, and then move on to the next one. You're not paralyzed by the thought of having to write an entire book all at once."

"Makes sense," I said, looking at my golf ball. Though my second shot wasn't anywhere near as spectacular as the first one, I somehow still managed to make it to the green. "So, let me get that straight; once you're clear on your end goal, all you need to do is take that daunting task and basically strip it down to a series of actionable steps?"

"That's right. And you can have the greatest plan in the world, but if you never take action on it, that's all it's ever going to be; a plan. So, let's say your goal is to bake a cake; your first cake. Well, instead of wasting time wondering how it's going to turn out, you should focus on the actual steps you need to take in order to make that cake." Jack had stopped walking and was now looking at me through his thick sunglasses.

"Sure, the end result may not look exactly like the picture," he continued. "And guess what; it may not taste like you thought it would either. But the only way to find out is to gather all your ingredients, and then follow the recipe. Not everything has to be perfect. If you allow yourself to fall into that trap, you'll never get anything done.

"Now, the same is also true for your book goal. Once you're clear on what it is that you want to accomplish, you need to get started somewhere. Just write the goddamn thing already! Start with a sentence, a paragraph; so long as you do something. It might take a little while before you get where you want to be, but if you're smart and you put in the work, trust me, you will get there. Just take that first step and you'll see."

Jack was right; the more involved you are in the overall process of turning your goals into a reality, the less time you have to worry about everything that could go wrong. All you need is to get started somewhere.

Chapter 16

"And then, you've got to make sure you don't forget *why* you're doing all this," he added.

I frowned.

"Well, I'm sure you've seen this before, but what happens with most people is that get started at something, ready to crush every obstacle, and then all of a sudden, when the hype starts to fade, they see their motivation go as well."

"I've seen it, but I've also experienced it firsthand," I said. "And more than once."

"That's because we humans tend to lose sight of our 'why' over time. We get caught up in our day-to-day lives, and as a result, we end up forgetting why we do what we do. Our focus gets sucked out at one point, and that's when we end up losing sight of our vision.

"And of course, you don't want that. You never want to lose sight of your vision, as this marks the beginning of a very slippery slope—"

"Really?" I thought out loud, interrupting him.

He smiled. "Well, let's say your goal is to get back in shape. You've been doing pretty well on your own over the past couple of weeks, running 30 minutes a day and eating healthy. But now that the initial excitement has faded away, how easy do you think it would be for you to skip a day or two? It's not like a 30-minute run really makes a difference anyway, right?"

Jack had made his point clear. "It may not seem like such a big deal at first, but something as subtle as allowing yourself to skip a day or two sets a precedent for you to skip a lot more days in the future," I slowly answered. "Making it a lot harder to create long-lasting good habits."

"Exactly. But people tend to forget about that, hence the importance of making sure that you never forget why you've taken action in the first place. So, why are you running? To get back in shape? Then this is what you've got to keep in mind. Never lose track of your 'why.' Ever."

"So, what do you suggest?"

"Easy; when you write down your goal, make sure you write down your 'why' along with it. In a journal if you have one, or on a piece of paper you can carry in your wallet; it's up to you. But again, be sure to put it somewhere you can see it every day."

I nodded. "And you have a journal?"

"Of course I do," Jack responded. "And I know what you're thinking right now. However, make no mistake; this has nothing to do with your typical teenage girl's diary. Every successful person I know keeps a journal—"

"Is that right?" I said, unable to hide my surprise.

"That's how they keep track of their goals. You should get one."

"I'll look into it. But regarding what you said earlier, I was wondering; what happens when you genuinely have no idea where to start? I mean, I know we've talked about excuses and all that stuff, but don't you feel like this can be a real struggle sometimes?"

He looked at me before he said anything. "Well, maybe your action plan is the real problem here. Maybe you simply haven't come up with the right actionable steps. Unfortunately, the only way to find out is to take a step back and go through the whole process all over again."

"And do you know what a good rule of thumb would be?"

"Depending on your goal, I'd say each step shouldn't take you more than a day or two to complete at the very most. If it takes you longer than that, maybe it's a sign you should consider breaking your goal into even smaller steps."

I nodded in silence, grabbing the putter in Jack's bag.

"And don't be too hard on yourself either," added the man as I stepped on the green. "We all have days where everything seems to go wrong for no reason; that's just how it goes. No need to beat yourself up. If your goal is to write 500 words a day and you end up writing only 100 on a bad day, be appreciative of that; at least you've done something."

He paused as I was getting ready to hit the ball.

"I guess what I'm saying is that some progress is better than no progress," Jack continued after I missed my first attempt. "I mean, when you think about it, a hundred words a day really isn't that bad after all. Not only is it better than doing nothing, but it also helps you build a strong and measurable momentum around your progress."

"A momentum?"

"Well, as I'm sure you remember, habits can be quite powerful when used to get things done the right way. That's because consistency tends to build up over time, creating momentum. And so, once you get the ball rolling, it makes it that much harder for you to give up."

"So, you want to make it a habit to work on your goals," I slowly repeated to myself, reaching for my phone. "Interesting. Let me write that down."

It was now Jack's turn to hit the green. I had lost my edge, but at that point, I was too busy trying to wrap my mind around everything he was saying for it to bother me.

"Now, on a cheerful note," Jack continued, "I think it's also very important that you learn how to celebrate the results you get. Because it's also part of the process to acknowledge what has been accomplished, right?"

Well, that was unexpected, I thought.

"Don't be so surprised," he said in a muted chuckle. "I've probably celebrated a lot more than you can imagine. There's a time to hustle, of course, but part of the fun is also to celebrate the small victories as they come.

What's important is that you know where to trace the line.

"And I'm not talking about getting drunk, staying up late and doing all the stupid things we do when we're young. I guess that's also part of a balanced life in a certain way, but I'm sure you already know everything there is to know about that."

I laughed.

"What I'm saying is that it's important to take a moment to really appreciate the results you've already gotten before you ask for more," Jack added. "Being grateful for what you already have will always serve you well; never forget that."

I nodded in silence.

"So, if I were to sum up the whole process for you, I'd say you need to plan your steps first, and then visualize and feel your success. Once you're done with all that preparation work, you focus on one of those steps and use what you've learned thus far to take action on it. Celebrate the outcome you get, and repeat."

"Anything else?" I asked as I was finishing writing down what he had just said.

Chapter 16

"I think that's it," he slowly answered. "So, what's your next move going to be?"

CHAPTER 17

After we finished our friendly round of golf, Jack and I went for a quick bite and headed back to his office, where I had left my car earlier in the morning.

"It might be a little while before you hear from me again," the man suddenly said as we pulled into the parking lot, speaking for the first time since we had left the diner. "I'll be traveling a lot in the upcoming weeks."

I nodded.

"I'll be in touch," he added, shaking my hand. "Take care, buddy."

Minutes later, I was back on the road, this time on my own, thinking about everything I had learned since my first encounter with Jack.

From more technical business advice to the simplest life lessons, the man had provided me with a variety of useful knowledge and wisdom—all of which would probably be engraved in my memory for years to come.

Among many other things, I had learned a lot about self-discipline, how to stay focused and how to get rid of my limiting beliefs.

Not only that, but he had also taught me how to embrace the mistakes I made and learn from them instead of running away. From there, I had learned how to cultivate a healthy mindset, how others can have an impact on me as well, positive or negative, but also how to set goals and take deliberate action on them.

And through our conversations, whether on the phone or in person, Jack had always been able to provide me with real-life examples to support his explanations. That's one thing I really liked about his teachings; the man knew how to keep things practical.

Becoming Jack's apprentice, I had had the incredible privilege to spend time with him and learn directly from his own experience.

And now, with all that new knowledge sinking in, I didn't really have a choice anymore; it was time for me to step up, leave my fears behind and start working on my dreams.

CHAPTER 18

A couple of days later I was up in my room, writing down my goals for the next quarter when all of a sudden, the doorbell rang. The man at the door handed me a thick FedEx envelope in exchange for a signature, politely wished me a very nice day and left me standing there as he walked back to his truck.

Closing the door behind me, I rushed to the kitchen and ripped the envelope open, revealing what appeared to be a journal—a fancy one—with a sticky note on it, reading:

"Figured you could use a little extra help to get started... That should do. —Jack."

At that point, I must admit, I was a little intrigued. Although it showed minor signs of wear and tear on the edges, the journal still seemed in pretty good shape. On the leather-wrapped front cover, the initials *J.O.* had been carefully embossed and filled with gold, an elegant touch that was complemented by a red ribbon attached on the inside of the spine. It was the kind of journal you would see proudly displayed on the corner of a president's desk.

Inside, folded notes and loose pieces of paper were stuck between every page or so, making the whole thing a lot thicker than it was originally intended to be.

Going through the first few pages, I noticed a bunch of goals that had already been crossed out, some of them dating all the way back to 2003. A little further in, I also found notes on all the concepts Jack and I had seen together, as well as a few other things like a bucket list, a bunch of detailed action plans and a list of principles to live by.

All in all, it took me just under two days to go through the entire journal, reading every single page and every single note from one cover to the other. And although it didn't really teach me anything new, it definitely helped me get a better understanding of what a journal really is for.

Because somehow, I always thought people used journals to keep track of their past and look back at what had already been accomplished. Whereas in reality, a journal is really more of an organizer for the things that are coming. It's a tool for growth.

And so, after reading the note Jack had left for me at the very end of his journal, saying, *"It's up to you to get started now..."* I drove to the store and bought one for myself on the very same day. When I got back home, I opened the notebook, put down the day's date and started writing.

I'm Mathieu Fortin, this is my journal, and my goal for this year is to...

THE END

ABOUT THE AUTHORS

About Mathieu...

MATHIEU FORTIN is a young author and entrepreneur. As a teenager, while most of his friends were doing homework and playing video games, Mathieu was already onto something else; reading everything he could find on business and personal growth.

By the age of 16, he had already launched his first online business, showing the world what a passion, a dream and a vision can accomplish when put together. Through the years, Mathieu has been involved in many different projects, going all the way from the automotive industry to the personal development field.

Today, he is focused on one thing; sharing the valuable knowledge he has learned over the past five years from his mentors and his own experience to help young aspiring entrepreneurs and artists turn their dreams into reality.

About Jack...

JACK OUNDJIAN was born in Yerevan, Armenia in 1981. Following his parents, his sister and his grandmother, he then moved to Montreal in 1988, where he grew up in a very modest environment.

Despite all that, and despite being timid on the surface, Jack went on to start multiple businesses in his early teens, which then led him to become a self-made millionaire by the age of 25.

Today, being a scholar in the automotive business and having an extensive knowledge of the real estate and forex markets, the man spends most of his time mentoring young professionals and playing chess.

ACKNOWLEDGMENTS

A note from Mathieu...

I would personally like to thank the man who took part in this project with me, my first real business mentor, Jack. Thank you for your teachings, and for always keeping faith in me.

A note from Jack...

I would like to thank my parents for giving me so much with so little available. Also, I would like to thank my grandmother, who spent countless hours teaching and showing me how the world works, without forgetting my wife Maria and my two boys who inspire me every single day.

www.ingramcontent.com/pod-product-compliance
Lightning Source LLC
Chambersburg PA
CBHW061648040426
42446CB00010B/1639